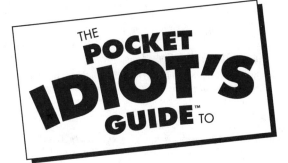

THE POCKET IDIOT'S GUIDE™ TO

Bartending

Second Edition

by Alan Axelrod and The Players

D0681064

ALPHA

A Pearson Education Company

For Anita—Here's looking at you, kid.

Contents

1 Garbage and Garnishes: 1
The Essential Equipment
of Bartending

2 Measuring, Mixing, and Pouring 17
Like a Pro

3 Brother Juniper: The Joys of Gin 29

4 Na Zdorovye! The Vorld of Vodka 45

5 The Silver Bullet Reloaded 57

6 Mostly Bourbon (and a Touch 69
of Tennessee)

7 Blends of Canada and the 85
Lower Forty-Eight

8 Comin' Through the Rye 101

9 Spirits of Thistle and Shamrock 113

10 Caribbean Sugar: A Rum Resumé 127

11 Tequila! 143

12 Liquid Luxuries: Brandies and 157
Liqueurs

13 Fires of Passion: Up in Flames: 175
Hot and Flaming Drinks

A Buzzed Word Glossary 191

B Last Call 201

Index 225

Introduction

The very last person who should pick up this *Pocket Idiot's Guide* is an idiot. These books are for people savvy and sensitive enough to feel like idiots about certain subjects. Most people find quantum physics an intimidating subject, but even more are snowed by mixology: the art and science of creating alcoholic—we prefer the term spiritous—beverages. What liquor to buy, what drinks to mix, how to measure them, how to mix them, how to pour them, how to serve them, and how to plan a party—these are bewilderments sufficient to reduce Albert Einstein himself to a quivering mass of Jell-O. (By the way, you will find recipes for splendid Jell-O shots in this *Pocket Idiot's Guide*.)

Extras

In addition to recipes, advice, guidance, and explanations, this book offers other types of information to help you mix drinks and enjoy the "pleasures of the spirit." These include definitions of key terms, tips from the world of professional bartending, a collection of popular toasts, and choice barroom humor. Look for these easy-to-recognize signposts in boxes:

Buzzed Words

The vocabulary of bartending, mixology, and liquor.

Toast

Toasts—popular, unique, sincere, funny.

Quick One

Barroom humor.

Bar Tips

Expert advice on the finer points of mixology.

Trademarks

All terms mentioned in this *Pocket Idiot's Guide* that are known to be or are suspected of being trademarks or service marks have been appropriately capitalized. Alpha Books and Pearson Education, Inc., cannot attest to the accuracy of this information. Use of a term in this book should not be regarded as affecting the validity of any trademark or service mark. The following trademarks and service marks have been mentioned in this book: 7-Up, Absolut, Angostura, Appleton, Asbach-Uralt, Bacardi and Company, Bailey's Original Irish Cream, Benedictine, Bermudez, British Navy Pusser's, Cacique Ron Añejo, Captain Morgan, Chartreuse, Cherry Marnier, Coca-Cola, Cointreau,

Dr. Pepper, Dubonnet, Finlandia, Glenfiddich, Glenmorangle, Grand Marnier, Hudson's Bay, Irish Mist, K.W.V., Knockando, Laphroaig, Lemon Hart & Sons, Macallan, Mandarine Napoleaon Liqueur, Metaxa, Midori, Mount Gay, Myer's Rum, Old Overholt, Pernod, Peter Heering, Peychaud's, Pisco, Presidente, Rhum Barbancourt, Ron Medellin, Rose's Lime Juice, Seagram's 7-Crown, Smirnoff, Stolichnaya, The Glenlivet, Tia Maria, Wyborowa, Zubrowka.

Chapter

Garbage and Garnishes: The Essential Equipment of Bartending

In This Chapter

- Stocking a basic liquor cabinet
- What you need for an advanced bar
- Mixers, basic and advanced
- Glassware and other equipment

There is no one "right" way to stock your bar. The liquor and equipment you select depend on your personal needs, your taste, what you and your friends enjoy, and your budget. This chapter gives you a range of suggestions, from bare bones to bells and whistles.

Bare Bones

At its most basic, the home bar can be a kitchen-cabinet collection of the two or three kinds of mixers and spirits you and your friends enjoy.

Liquors

Below are the basics for a "starter bar":

- Bourbon
- Canadian whisky
- Blended scotch
- Gin
- Light rum
- White tequila
- Vodka
- Brandy

Liqueurs

Even a basic bar should stock small bottles of the most popular liqueurs. Include at least four of the following:

- Triple sec
- Crème de menthe
- Crème de cacao
- Amaretto
- Kahlua
- Drambuie
- Benedictine
- Cointreau
- Grand Marnier

Wine and Beer

For the "starter bar," stock the following:

- Dry vermouth
- Sweet vermouth
- White wine
- Red wine
- Champagne or sparkling wine
- Beer/light beer

Mixers

You will want to stock six carbonated mixers.

These mix well with light alcohols, such as gin, vodka, and rum:

- Cola
- Diet cola
- Tonic water

For the dark spirits—such as scotch and bourbon—have on hand the following:

- Club soda
- Ginger ale
- 7-Up (or the equivalent)

You'll also need five basic juices. If possible, purchase them just before use, so that they'll be fresh:

- Orange juice
- Grapefruit juice
- Pineapple juice
- Cranberry juice
- Tomato juice

A number of drinks call for *sour mix* or *bar mix* (which is the same thing). You can buy this bottled or in ready-to-mix powdered form at liquor stores or grocery stores. If you prefer, you can prepare it yourself. There are two basic recipes.

Sour Mix Recipe 1

Juice of $1/2$ lemon per drink

1 tsp. sugar per drink

Simply combine these with other drink ingredients in a shaker with ice. Shake vigorously.

Commercial powdered sour mix adds powdered egg white to the product to make the drink foam up. If you shake the cocktail vigorously, you shouldn't need the egg white; however, if you want to ensure a really foamy sour, try this recipe:

Sour Mix Recipe 2

12 oz. lemon juice (the juice of 6 lemons)

18 oz. distilled water

$1/4$ cup refined sugar

1 egg white

Blend all ingredients in a blender.
Refrigerate.

Note: The mix will keep for about a week under refrigeration. You must shake or blend it before each use.

Round out your "starter bar" basic mixer arsenal with these:

- 1 small bottle of Rose's lime juice
- Superfine granulated sugar

- Coarse (not table) salt (for margaritas and Salty Dogs)
- Grenadine
- Sugar syrup (also known as simple syrup)

Bar Tips _____

You can buy sugar syrup ready-made or prepare it at home. In a saucepan, gradually dissolve 2 cups of sugar in a cup of water. Simmer for 10 minutes, stirring frequently. Refrigerate until needed.

One Step Beyond

If "bare bones" doesn't make it for you, here's the next logical step. To the "starter bar," add the following spirits:

- Dutch (Genever) gin
- A flavor-infused gin or two
- English gin
- Scandinavian or Russian vodka
- A flavor-infused vodka or two
- Rye
- Irish whiskey
- Single-malt scotch
- Bourbon or Tennessee whiskey
- Gold rum
- Dark (Jamaican) rum
- Gold tequila (*tequila añejo*)

Bar Tips

Several major distillers of gin and vodka now offer their products infused with orange, mint, and lime (for gins) and a wide variety of fruits and spices (for vodkas). If you haven't been keeping up with what's available, check out any well-supplied liquor store.

There is a wide range of exotic liqueurs available. Consider the following additions to the basic roster:

- Crème de cassis
- Sambuca
- Peppermint schnapps
- Peach schnapps
- Galliano
- Frangelico

You can add any number of great wines and beers to your collection. Do consider the following:

- Aperitif wines (Dubonnet, Lillet, and Campari are the most popular)
- Cream sherry
- Port
- Madeira
- Amontillado

Get at least two or three flavored brandies:

- Calvados or applejack (apple brandy)
- Apricot brandy
- Peach brandy

In addition to the most-requested mixers, you might also keep on hand the following:

- Coffee
- Cream (heavy and light)
- Cream of coconut
- Bitters

Buzzed Words

Bitters is an *alcoholic* mixer (Angostura bitters is the best known) that gives a special piquance to Manhattans, old-fashioneds, and even Bloody Marys. Because bitters contains alcohol, never use it to flavor nonalcoholic drinks for nondrinkers.

Garnishes and Garbage

Many mixed drinks have solid as well as liquid components. If a piece of fruit or vegetable added to a drink changes the way it tastes, then it is called a *garnish*. If it's just for decoration, it's *garbage*. These are the terms professional bartenders use.

The basic bar should have the following garnishes and garbage available:

Lemon twists   All you use is the peel. The way to get the most peel from each lemon is to slice off the ends, and then use a spoon to force the fruit out one end. Now you have an empty lemon peel. Slice it lengthwise into strips 1/4 inch wide. When a drink calls for a "twist," take one of the strips, twist it over the drink, rub the inside of the peel around the edge of the glass, plunk it in, and then stir.

Lime wedges   Unlike lemons, limes are rarely cut into twist strips; cut them into wedges.

Orange slices   Resist the temptation to squeeze the orange into the drink.

Maraschino cherries   These super-sweet, surrealistically red-dyed little numbers are garbage; that is, they add no flavor to the drink. However, drinkers like to pull them out of the drink and eat them, so make certain you leave the stems on.

Olives   Most martini drinkers like their libation with an olive or three. Use medium-size green pitted olives. Some drinkers don't like pimento in their olives because it may discolor the drink. Usually, the olive(s) are skewered on a toothpick or a little plastic sword and placed in the drink.

Pearl onions   A martini harboring a pearl onion (or two or three) rather than an olive or olives is more properly called a Gibson. Stored under refrigeration in its own juice, this garnish will keep indefinitely. The pearls may be skewered on a toothpick.

Celery stalks   These add the finishing touch to a Bloody Mary. To add some flair, leave the stalk's leafy end on.

Buzzed Words

A **garnish** is a bit of fruit or vegetable added to a drink principally to enhance its flavor. **Garbage** is a bit of fruit or vegetable added to a drink primarily for the sake of appearance. It does not significantly enhance the flavor of the drink.

Accessories

Don't forget cocktail toothpicks or, if you yearn for a dash of kitsch, little plastic cocktail swords. You'll also need swizzle sticks or cocktail straws.

Tools of the Trade

There's a load of gadgets and glassware a bartender can buy. Some of them are even useful.

Shaker Upper

The trademark of the pro is the cocktail shaker. You'll need one to make sours, daiquiris, margaritas, and a straight-up martini à la James Bond ("shaken, not stirred"). Buy one with a stainless-steel shell—the bigger, outer part—and glass, the smaller, inner part. A 12-ounce shaker should be ample.

You'll also need a cocktail strainer that fits over the shaker so that you can pour the chilled drink without disgorging the ice cubes. This is called pouring a drink "straight up."

Other (More or Less) Essentials

If you're going for that pro look, you'll also want a number of *speedpourers*—the plastic gadgets that fit into the mouth of a liquor bottle, enabling you to pour the liquor at an even, measured rate without spilling.

While you're at it, why not buy a genuine *bar spoon*? This has a small paddle spoon at one end of a long handle that is twisted in the middle. The spoon is the bartender's Swiss army knife: Drinks can be stirred with the handle, garnishes can be manipulated with the spoon (if you don't want to use your fingers), and the swirled part can be used to pour the ingredients of layered drinks—such as pousse-cafés—in which it is important to avoid blending the layers.

Here is other equipment you are likely to have in your kitchen already:

- A paring knife for cutting fruit garnishes
- A cutting board—to make for neater cutting
- An electric blender
- An ice bucket with ice tongs (for the fastidious)

A Glass Act

Glassware is far less critical in serving liquor than it is in serving fine wine. However, glass size and shape can enhance or detract from the experience of enjoying straight liquor as well as mixed drinks. Let's go over the basics.

Highball and Low

The *highball glass* is the one you'll use most. High-ball glasses are used for scotch and soda, bourbon and water, gin and tonic—you get the picture. The orthodox highball glass is a tall 8 ounces; however, some more ambitious glasses hold 12 ounces.

Only slightly less popular is the *lowball glass*, which some bartenders call a *rocks glass*, since it is used for many drinks served on the rocks. Ranging from 4 to 9 ounces, this short, clear glass is used for martinis on the rocks, various whiskey-rocks combinations, Manhattans on the rocks, and so on.

Collins and Old-Fashioned

The *Collins glass* is not just for the Tom Collins, but for any of the larger mixed drinks that benefit from a cooling, refreshing image. This includes the various fizzes and a wealth of tropical drinks. The 10- to 14-ounce Collins glass is frosted (sometimes with an icy pebble effect as well) to about ³/₄" from the top.

Old-fashioned glasses come in two sizes, large (7-ounce) and small (4-ounce), and are similar to the lowball glass, except for the bump at the base of the glass. Presumably, this is to remind the bartender to prepare the fixings for the old-fashioned.

> **Bar Tips**
>
> The Collins glass would be the same as a large (12-ounce) highball glass, except that the highball glass is entirely clear, whereas the Collins glass is partially frosted.

Cocktail and Sour

The classic *cocktail glass* is so classic—an inverted cone perched on a long stem—that it is, quite literally, *the* icon of the cocktail lounge, often immortalized in neon signs. The 4-ounce glass is used for any cocktail ordered straight up. Its stem is more than decorative: Since drinks served in cocktail glasses have no ice in them, the stem enables you to hold the glass without warming the contents with your hands. You might add a few 4- or 5-ounce *sour glasses* to your collection. These are stemmed glasses with elongated bowls that make whiskey sours (and other foamy sour drinks) more inviting.

Wine and Sherry

The subject of wine glasses is complex. If you enjoy fine wines, read *The Complete Idiot's Guide to Wine*, which includes a discussion of glassware. For the basic bar, however, the sturdy, stemmed, globe-bowled glasses of a Parisian-style bistro are adequate.

You may also stock some *sherry glasses*. These 2½- to 3½-ounce stemmed glasses can be used for aperitifs and port as well as for sherry. The best kind of sherry glass is the *copita*, which features a narrow taper that captures the wine's aroma. If you prefer, however, you may serve these drinks in the smaller *pony* or *cordial* glasses.

Champagne: American Style and in a European Mood

Americans tend to favor a stemmed glass that looks like a shorter, wider, shallower version of the cocktail glass. It holds 4 to 6 ounces of bubbly. Europeans, however, prefer a very different glass, the champagne flute, which is tall and fluted—bulging gracefully at the bottom and tapering toward the rim.

Swallow your patriotism before you swallow your champagne; choose the European flute over the American champagne glass. Not only does it hold more of a good thing (capacities vary from 7 to 11 ounces), but, more important, its tapered profile reduces the surface area of the liquid, which slows the dissipation of the bubbles. The champagne stays fresher longer.

Bar Tips _____

Using champagne flutes results in less spillage than American-style champagne glasses.

Small Is Beautiful: Pony and Shot

Every bar should have a supply of shot glasses, which you can use not only to serve shots, but also to measure drinks. Shot glasses come in 1- to 2-ounce sizes, and your wisest choice is 1½ ounces—a *jigger*—because this is the ideal size for measuring most drinks.

Buzzed Words _____

A **jigger** is the glass or the metal measuring cup used to measure drinks. It is also what you call the amount the jigger measures: 1½ ounces. Strictly speaking, a pony is a 1-ounce measure; however, pony glasses range in capacity from 1 to 2 ounces.

Snifter Story

The *brandy snifter* is a particularly elegant piece of glassware. It ranges in capacity anywhere from about 5 to 25 ounces; however, no snifter is meant to hold so vast an amount of brandy. Opt for about a 16-ounce snifter, in which you serve no more than 1 or 2 ounces of brandy. The idea is that the oversized balloon shape of the snifter will waft and funnel the aroma of the wine into the drinker's nose. If you use a snifter smaller than 16 ounces, reduce the amount of brandy proportionately.

Mugs and Pilsner Glasses

Should you choose mugs, pilsner glasses, or both? Mugs won't break as easily, but if you are serving really wonderful premium beer, the tall, elegant *pilsner glass* can enhance the drinking experience. It's your call. In either case, drinking beer from a mug or glass is far more enjoyable than sucking on a bottle or slurping from a can.

Other Specialized Glassware

Now that you've had a rundown of the basic bar glassware, you should also know about the following specialized glasses:

- **Pousse-café glass**   A 3- to 4-ounce stemmed glass with little or no flare or tapering of the bowl. It is handy for layered dessert drinks.

- **Parfait glass**   A slightly larger version of the pousse-café glass, the parfait glass usually has a flared lip. It is also used for layered dessert drinks.

- **Fizz glass**   This 5-ounce stemmed glass is shorter but wider than a 5-ounce sour glass. It is useful if you want to serve fizz drinks in something smaller than a Collins glass.

- **Martini glass** Some people prefer their martini in this modified version of a cocktail glass rather than in a cocktail glass. Typically 4 ounces, the martini glass tapers to a very shallow point at the stem, unlike the cocktail glass, which tapers to an acute point.
- **Eggnog mug** This large, barrel-shaped mug is a fun way to enjoy eggnog drinks.

Do you really need any of these specialized items? Base your decisions on your taste, on what you and your guests like to drink, and on just how "complete" a host/bartender you want (and can afford) to be.

Chapter 2

Measuring, Mixing, and Pouring Like a Pro

In This Chapter

- The three basic kinds of drinks
- Methods of measuring
- When (and how) to stir; when (and how) to shake
- Pouring like a pro
- Preparing your glassware

If you've comparison-shopped before buying this book—or if you've been mistrustful enough to consult another book after purchasing this one (shame on you!)—you may have been overwhelmed by the sheer number of drinks it is possible to mix.

Take a deep breath. The fact is, almost all of those hundreds, even thousands, of "different" drinks are really variations on three basic themes: the highball, the stirred cocktail ("lowball"), and the shaken cocktail. Master the themes, and you'll have no trouble with the variations. This chapter will show you how.

Highball Architecture

Don't just mix a drink. *Build* one. And as any architect knows, all great buildings begin with a firm foundation—in this case, rocks. Start with ice, which should occupy about two thirds of a highball glass.

Bar Tips _____

Buy one pound of ice per guest at a four-hour party, unless you know it's primarily a beer-and-wine crowd.

Get Jiggered with It

Having laid your foundation, pour in one jigger (that is, 1½ ounces) of liquor. Either use a jigger measure or a jigger-size shot glass. Then pour in the mixer—right to the top. Not only will this give you the proper liquor-to-mixer proportion for taste, it also *looks* generous. Most important, it will keep you from mixing your drinks too strong. Your object is to dispense enjoyment, not intoxication.

If the mixer is carbonated, your work is done (unless the drink calls for the addition of a garnish) because the bubbles, not you, do the mixing. In fact, resist the temptation to stir. Doing so will only accelerate the dissipation of the bubbles, and the drink will taste flat.

If the mixer is noncarbonated, either give the drink a few quick stirs with your bar spoon or just put a straw in the glass and let the drinker stir to his or her heart's content.

Two Fingers or Three Counts

Measuring with a jigger is accurate, but slow—and it may make you look stingy. Faster is the two-finger measure. Just wrap two fingers around the bottom of the glass and pour the liquor until it reaches the top of the top finger.

If you use a speedpourer (see the previous chapter), which provides a steady, controllable, even flow of liquor, you might want to use the Three-Count Technique. Here's how to do it:

1. After filling a highball glass two thirds with ice, grab the liquor bottle firmly by the neck. The bottle *must* have a speedpourer inserted!

2. In a single, quick motion, invert the bottle—*completely upside down*—over the glass.

3. Count to three. (Not out loud. And don't move your lips.)

Practice this maneuver until your three count ("one-thousand one, one-thousand two, one-thousand three …") dispenses 1½ ounces. Why bother with the Three-Count? It is a virtuoso method that makes you look like a pro. Besides, once you've got it down, you won't even have to think about counting. Your sense of timing will kick in, and the result will be effortless and rapid drink preparation.

Bar Tips _____

It pays to practice the Three-Count Technique. Once you match three counts with a 1½-ounce pour, you can match one count to a ½ ounce—and four counts will give you 2 ounces—should you ever need to deviate from the standard jigger. For practice purposes, water is best.

Shaken—or Stirred?

So, what's the big deal when Agent 007 suavely orders his martini, specifying that it be "shaken, not stirred"? It's unorthodox, that's what. It's bold and daring—as befits a secret agent licensed to kill.

The classic martini is stirred, not shaken. Arguably, shaking rather than stirring the martini "improves" its taste by aerating the drink. Maybe. But it also may cloud the martini with tiny air bubbles—not aesthetically pleasing. Here's the accepted rule of thumb: If a drink consists of clear, relatively thin ingredients (such as the gin and vermouth of a martini), use the "least invasive" blending method—that is, stirring. If, however, a drink contains thicker fluids, such as fruit juice, shaking is required to blend the drink properly.

Toast _____

May you live as long as you want to, and want to as long as you live.

Like all rules, this one's meant to be broken. If your guest asks you to shake, shake. If stirring's requested, stir away.

Stirring a Lowball

Stirred cocktails may be prepared on the rocks or straight up. Let's walk through the mixing of a vodka gimlet as an example of a stirred cocktail prepared and served on the rocks:

1. Fill a lowball glass almost to the rim with ice.
2. Pour in 2 ounces of vodka.
3. Add ¼ ounce of Rose's lime juice.
4. Stir *well.*
5. Garnish with a lime wedge; drop it in.

That's one way to do it. You can also prepare on-the-rocks, stirred cocktails in a two-step process. Another vodka gimlet, please:

1. Fill a shaker glass (the small, inner part of a cocktail shaker) two thirds with ice.
2. Add 1 ounce of Rose's lime juice.
3. Pour in 5 ounces of vodka.
4. Stir vigorously. The objective is to let the ice thoroughly chill the drink.
5. Strain the gimlet into a single lowball glass large enough to accommodate it—or divide the drink between two smaller lowball glasses.
6. Garnish with a lime wedge.

The process of making a drink straight up is identical to the two-step method of preparing a drink on the rocks except that, instead of straining the chilled drink into a glass filled with ice, you just pour it into an empty, preferably chilled, glass. The key step is stirring vigorously and for a generous span of time—perhaps a count of 10 or 15. The drink really has to chill.

Great Shakes

Serious bartenders have always taken great pride in the panache with which they wield the cocktail shaker. And, despite the risk of catastrophic spillage, the secret is to be bold, vigorous—aggressive, even. Shake *hard*.

The following is the procedure for shaking a classic shaken drink, the whiskey sour:

1. Into a shaker glass two-thirds full of ice, pour 2 ounces of Canadian whisky.

2. Add 1¹/₂ ounces of sour mix.

3. Take the stainless steel shell of the cocktail shaker and put it on top of the glass. Press down *firmly* in order to create a leak-proof seal. The beauty of the steel shell is that it will contract during shaking, because the icy fluid lowers its temperature.

4. Use both hands. Put one hand on top of the shaker, and the other on the bottom. Grasp firmly. Shake hard for at least six counts.

5. If you've done everything right, the laws of physics will have created a stout seal between

the stainless steel top and the glass bottom of the shaker. To break the seal, so that you can get at the drink, look for the frost line on the steel shell. That's where the top and bottom are sealed. Firmly tap this line with the heel of your hand. You should hear a snap—that's the seal breaking.

6. The shell will now come off very easily. *But don't take it off yet.* First turn the shaker over, so that the steel shell is on the bottom. This will prevent spillage. *Now* take the glass out.

7. Strain the drink from the steel shell into a lowball glass or, if you have one, into a whiskey-sour glass. The advantage of the whiskey-sour glass is that, if the drinker handles it by the stem, the straight-up drink will stay colder longer.

8. Garnish. The classic finishing touches are a maraschino cherry inside the glass and an orange or lemon slice perched on the lip of the glass.

There is a downside to shaken drinks: the clean-up. Unless you are making one right after the other of the same drink, you'll need to clean the shaker immediately. It will get gummy and nasty if you don't. Rinse it with water; then wipe it out.

 **Quick One** _____

There was a college that had the reputation of being a fountain of knowledge. Everyone went there to drink.

Mix, Blend, and Puree!

Given a shaker and sufficient elbow grease, shaking is sufficient to blend most drinks. However, if you want to prepare frozen drinks, such as a frozen margarita, a frozen daiquiri, or a frozen piña colada, you'll need an electric blender.

First, be certain that your blender is up to the task of handling ice. A heavy-duty model is best. Then ...

1. Check to ensure that the motor is off. Pour the liquor into the blender. Next comes the mixers, and then the fruit. Last, add ice—enough to fill the blender to three-quarters full.

2. Make sure you put the lid on properly. Hold it down with one hand and start the machine at low speed. Once the initial mixing is complete, switch to high until everything is thoroughly blended.

3. Pour the drink directly into glasses. No straining is necessary because the ice has been crushed and blended with the drink.

Buzzed Words

Frozen drinks are also called **freezes**.

The Virtuoso Touch

There is great satisfaction in doing a job well—and that goes for bartending as well as anything else you do. Here are some expert tips and techniques for enhancing the satisfaction you take in serving your guests as well as their enjoyment in being served graciously.

Popping Your Cork

To open wine, begin by completely removing the foil "capsule" from the top of the bottle. If you are using the popular waiter's corkscrew, insert the point of the helical screw (called a "worm") into the cork slightly off center. Bore deeply into the cork, and then pull straight up, twisting slightly to loosen the cork. An easier alternative is to use either a twin-lever corkscrew or a screwpull-type corkscrew. These are available in most stores that sell food-preparation utensils.

Opening champagne is at once easier and more challenging than opening a bottle of wine. It's easier because you don't have to use a corkscrew. It's more challenging because the contents of the bottle are under great pressure.

- Inspect the bottle before opening it. Look for deep scratches or nicks. Deep imperfections in the glass may cause the bottle to explode.

- Do not chill champagne below 45 degrees. Chilling below this temperature increases the potential for an explosion.

- During the uncorking process, point the bottle away from you and others.

To remove the cork, point the bottle away from you and others, and remove the foil "capsule" covering the top. Next, untwist the wire cage that traps the cork. While doing this, place your palm over the cork to keep it from shooting out of the bottle. Now, still pointing the bottle away from all living beings, gently twist the cork, cupping your palm over it. As the cork works free, it will press against your palm. Do not release the cork. Do not let it pop. It should clear the bottle with a barely audible hiss (called by corny connoisseurs the "lover's sigh") or a muffled pop.

Using the Speedpourer

We've already discussed the speedpourer as absolutely required for bartenders using the Three-Count Method. Even if you don't use that method, however, speedpourers make your job neater and quicker—just be sure you take enough time to put the speedpourer in the bottle so that the slant of the mouth is at a right angle to the label. This will put more speed into your pour by enabling you to grab the bottle without having to check which way the stream of liquor will emerge. Moreover, your guests will be able to see the label as you pour—a nice touch, especially if you are serving premium liquor.

Developing a Multiple Personality

If you've admired the aplomb of the super-fast bartender who can prepare multiples of the same drink simultaneously, now is your chance to start admiring yourself. *You* can do it!

Just line up X number of glasses in a row. They should be filled with ice, and they should be standing rim to rim. Make sure a speedpourer is in the bottle of booze. Grab the bottle by the neck. Do a smooth inversion over the first glass, count three, move the still-inverted bottle smoothly to the next glass, count three, go on and on and on.

Unfortunately, because you can't put a speedpourer into most mixer bottles, you'll have to pour this ingredient in one glass at a time. Same goes for dispensing the garnish.

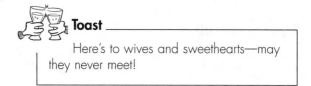

Toast

Here's to wives and sweethearts—may they never meet!

Chilling

If you want to chill a glass before pouring a drink into it, refrigerate the dry glass for an hour or longer, and then fill the glass with ice water. Prepare the drink. When you are ready to pour the drink, dump out the ice water.

Frosting

Frosting is a step beyond chilling. Dip the glass in water, and then put it in the freezer for one half an hour. This will give it a frosty white appearance. If the glass has a stem, hold it by the stem to avoid melting any of the frost.

Salting

Salting means rimming the glass with salt—something you may want to do for a Salty Dog or a margarita. It's easy if you remember to use rock salt rather than table salt.

Pour rock salt onto a plate. Take a lime wedge and rub it around the rim of the glass. Roll the glass rim around in the salt.

But before you do any of this, ask your guest if he or she *wants* the rim salted. Some drinkers don't like it.

Flavoring the Rim

Aside from salting, you can flavor the rim of any glass with the fruit used to garnish the drink. Just run the orange, lime, or lemon peel on the rim. It will impart a subtle flavor and aroma to the drink.

A few specialty drinks may be rimmed with sugar, cinnamon, and even cocoa. In these cases, it is usually sufficient to moisten the rim with a little of the main liquor ingredient in the drink, then roll the glass in a plate of the flavoring.

 Bar Tips

Tips on preparing lemon twists, lime wedges, orange slices, and other garnishes and "garbage" are found in Chapter 1.

Brother Juniper: The Joys of Gin

In This Chapter

- The flavorfulness of gin
- The variety of gin
- Gin recipes

A deeply aromatic spirit, gin doesn't appeal to everybody, but those who admire it cherish its bracing, refreshing qualities, redolent of juniper berries and a host of other botanicals—an often exotic collection of extracts from roots, barks, seeds, and leaves—that give gin its character. Unlike vodka, which is (or should be) flavorless, the character of gin varies greatly from brand to brand and invites a lot of "comparison shopping."

Variations on a Good Theme

There are lots of good gins out there, each with its own character, so feel free to experiment. A good place to start is with the three major premium brands: Beefeater, Tanqueray, and Bombay.

Beefeater is the most neutrally flavored of the three, Bombay the spiciest, and Tanqueray somewhere in between. After trying all three, you might use them as a benchmark for judging the flavor of other gins.

Buzzed Words

Gins are often designated **dry gin** or **London dry gin**. These originated when "sweet" (called **Old Tom**) as well as "dry" gin was available. Today, the distinction is mainly superfluous, because almost all English and American gin is now dry. Also note that London dry gin doesn't have to be made in London or even England. This describes a manufacturing style, not a place of origin.

Beefeater, Tanqueray, and Bombay are London-style gins. Far less familiar are the Dutch, or genever, gins. You may have to visit one of the larger liquor stores to find *any* Dutch gin, let alone more than a single brand. But it's worth the trip. This is a chance to find out what "original" gin is, as invented in the seventeenth century by Franciscus de la Boe, better known as Franciscus Sylvius, who distilled it as a diuretic tonic for Dutch soldiers.

Gin and ...

Although not everyone likes the taste of gin by itself, it vies with vodka as the most mixable of spirits. It can be combined with just about anything.

Gin and Bitters

*Serve straight up, strained into an
old-fashioned or lowball glass.*

2 oz. gin

$^1/_2$ tsp. Angostura bitters

Stir gin and bitters in a glass with ice cubes
until well chilled. Strain into the serving glass.

Gin and Campari

Serve in a lowball glass.

$1^1/_2$ oz. gin

$1^1/_2$ oz. Campari

Orange slice or twist of orange

Combine gin and Campari in a cocktail shaker
with ice. Shake vigorously, and then strain into
the serving glass filled with ice. Garnish with
orange slice or twist of orange.

Bar Tips

An open bottle of tonic water or club
soda is only good for about a day. To make
sure they're always bubbly, consider buying
them in six packs of small bottles, which you
can finish before they get flat. For a big
party, go for the larger bottles.

Gin and Sin

Serve straight up, strained into a cocktail glass.

2 oz. gin

1 TB. Cinzano

Combine gin and Cinzano in a glass with ice, stir until well chilled, and then strain into the serving glass.

Gin and Ginger

Serve on the rocks in a chilled highball glass.

$1^1/_2$ oz. gin

Ginger ale to fill

Lemon twist

Combine gin and ginger ale in the serving glass filled with ice. Drop in lemon twist.

Negroni

Serve straight up in a chilled cocktail glass.

2 oz. gin

$^1/_2$ oz. sweet vermouth

$^3/_4$ oz. Campari

Splash of club soda (optional)

Orange peel

Combine all ingredients, except orange peel, in a shaker with ice. Shake vigorously, and then strain into the serving glass. Twist orange peel and drop into the glass.

Gin and Soda

Serve on the rocks in a highball glass.

1¹/₂–2 oz. gin

Club soda to fill

Lemon twist

Pour gin into the serving glass filled with ice. Add club soda, and garnish with lemon twist.

Gin and Tonic

Serve on the rocks in a highball glass.

2–2¹/₂ oz. gin

Tonic water to fill

Lime wedge or lemon twist

Pour gin into the serving glass filled with ice. Add tonic, and garnish with lime wedge (traditional) or, if you prefer, lemon twist.

Bar Tips _____

Don't look for a martini here. It gets its own chapter: Chapter 5.

Gimlet Eye

The primary dictionary meaning of *gimlet* is a sharp tool for piercing. As a drink, a "gimlet" combines gin (or vodka) with lime or lemon juice to provide something of a piercing pick-me-up.

Gimlet with Fresh Lime

Serve in a chilled old-fashioned or lowball glass.

2 oz. gin

$^1/_2$ oz. fresh lime (or limon) juice

Lime twist or lime slice

Stir gin and juice very vigorously in a mixing (shaker) glass with cracked ice; pour into the serving glass. Garnish with lime twist or lime slice. May also be served straight up: Stir with ice cubes, and then strain into the serving glass.

Gimlet with Rose's Lime Juice

Serve in a chilled old-fashioned or lowball glass.

2 oz. gin

$^1/_2$ oz. Rose's lime juice

Lime slice

Use a shaker or blender to mix gin and Rose's with cracked ice; pour into the serving glass. The best garnish is a lime slice, which gets more of the natural juice into the drink. May also be served straight up: Strain the shaken or blended ingredients into the serving glass.

Tom Collins

Serve on the rocks in a Collins or highball glass.

2–3 oz. gin

1¹/₂ oz. lemon juice

1¹/₂ oz. sugar syrup

Club soda to fill

Maraschino cherry

Combine all ingredients except club soda and cherry in the serving glass with ice. Stir well. Fill with club soda, and garnish with cherry.

Juices (Mostly)

Most of us are familiar with vodka and orange juice (the screwdriver) and with vodka and grapefruit juice. No law says you can't substitute gin for vodka in these faithful standbys.

Gin Screwdriver

Serve on the rocks in a highball glass.

1¹/₂ oz. gin

2–3 oz. orange juice

Stir well. If you like, add a dash or two of Angostura bitters.

Orange Blossom

Serve in a chilled cocktail glass.

1¹/₂ oz. gin

1 oz. orange juice

Orange slice

Combine all ingredients, except orange slice, in a shaker with ice. Shake vigorously, and then strain into the serving glass. Garnish with orange slice.

Abbey

Serve on the rocks in a lowball glass.

1¹/₂ oz. gin

1¹/₂ oz. orange juice

Dash or two of orange bitters

Maraschino cherry

Combine all ingredients, except for cherry, in a shaker with ice. Shake vigorously, and then strain into the ice-filled serving glass. Garnish with cherry.

Bronx Cocktail

Serve straight up in a chilled cocktail glass.

1$\frac{1}{2}$ oz. gin

$\frac{1}{2}$ oz. orange juice

Dash of dry vermouth

Dash of sweet vermouth

Combine all ingredients, with ice, in a shaker. Shake vigorously. Strain into the serving glass. Some drinkers prefer more of the vermouths— $\frac{1}{2}$ ounce each—and a full ounce of orange juice. If you want a dry cocktail, skip the sweet vermouth.

Atomic Bomb

Serve on ice in a lowball glass.

2 oz. gin

1 oz. Benedictine

4 dashes curaçao

Combine all ingredients in a lowball glass, about one third filled with ice.

Abbey Cocktail

Serve straight up in a chilled cocktail glass.

1¹/₂ oz. gin

¹/₄ oz. orange juice

³/₄ oz. sweet vermouth

Dash or 2 of Angostura bitters

Maraschino cherry

Combine all ingredients, except for cherry, in a shaker with ice. Shake vigorously, and then strain into the serving glass. Garnish with cherry.

Gin Sour

Serve straight up in a whiskey sour glass or lowball glass.

2–3 oz. gin

1 oz. lemon juice

1 tsp. sugar syrup

Orange or lemon slice

Maraschino cherry

In a shaker, with ice, combine all ingredients except garnishes. Shake vigorously. Strain into the serving glass. Garnish with orange slice and maraschino cherry.

Fizz, Rickey, Daisy, and a Sidecar

A fizz is cousin to a Collins and always includes club soda. A *rickey* is a fizz with lime, and a daisy is a fizz sweetened up to the max. The origin of the name "sidecar" is a mystery, but making one is quite simple.

Buzzed Words

A **rickey** is any drink with soda water and lime—and sometimes sugar.

Gin Fizz

Serve on the rocks in a Collins or tall highball glass.

1½ oz. gin

1 TB. powdered sugar

3 oz. sour mix

Club soda to fill

Maraschino cherry

Orange slice

To a shaker filled with ice add gin, sugar, and sour mix. Shake vigorously. Pour into the ice-filled serving glass, and then add club soda. Garnish with maraschino cherry and orange slice.

Gin Daisy

Serve in a chilled highball glass.

2–3 oz. gin

1 oz. lemon juice

$1/4$ oz. raspberry syrup or grenadine

$1/2$ tsp. sugar syrup

Club soda to fill

Orange slice

To a shaker filled with cracked ice add all ingredients except for club soda and orange slice. Shake vigorously. Pour into the serving glass. Add club soda to fill, and then garnish with orange slice.

Gin Rickey

Serve on the rocks in a highball glass.

$1^1/2$ oz. gin

Club soda to fill

Juice of $1/2$ fresh lime

Fill a highball glass half full of ice cubes; pour in gin, and then club soda to fill. Add lime juice.

Gin Sidecar

Serve in a chilled old-fashioned or lowball glass.

1½ oz. gin

¾ oz. triple sec

1 oz. lemon juice

Pour all ingredients into a shaker with cracked ice. Shake vigorously. Pour into the serving glass.

Liqueur Refreshed and a Sling Reslung

Liqueur: heavy, sweet, and ideal for dessert drinks. That's a true assessment as far as it goes, but, if you know how to combine gin and liqueur, you'll see that this truism just doesn't go far enough. Neither liqueur nor flavored brandy need be reserved just for desserts.

Cornell Cocktail

Serve straight up in a chilled cocktail glass.

4 oz. gin

1 oz. Maraschino liqueur

1 egg white*

Vigorously shake all ingredients with ice in a shaker, or blend; strain into the serving glasses. Recipe makes two drinks.

---

* *Raw egg may be a source of salmonella bacteria. You may wish to avoid drinks calling for raw egg yolk or egg white.*

Slings are sweet drinks made with brandy, whiskey, or gin. Here's the gin version.

Coco Chanel

Serve straight up in a chilled cocktail glass.

1 oz. gin

1 oz. Kahlua or Tia Maria

1 oz. heavy cream

In a shaker or blender, mix all ingredients with cracked ice. Strain into a chilled cocktail glass.

Gin Sling

Serve in an old-fashioned or lowball glass.

2–3 oz. gin

1 oz. lemon juice

$1/2$ oz. orgeat or sugar syrup

Club soda to fill

Fill a serving glass half full with cracked ice. Add all ingredients except club soda. Stir. Add club soda to fill. If you don't want a fizzy drink, substitute plain water for club soda.

A Tropical Pedigree

Gin may have been popularized in chilly lanes of jolly old London, but it's also a natural in drinks appropriate to tropic climates.

Bermuda Cocktail

Serve in a chilled old-fashioned or lowball glass.

1$\frac{1}{2}$ oz. gin

1 oz. apricot brandy

$\frac{1}{2}$ oz. lime juice (fresh or Rose's)

1 tsp. Falernum or sugar syrup

Dash of grenadine

Orange peel

$\frac{1}{2}$ tsp. curaçao

To a shaker filled with cracked ice add all ingredients except orange peel and curaçao. Shake vigorously. Pour into the serving glass. Garnish with orange peel twist; then carefully top with curaçao so that it floats.

Singapore Sling

Serve on the rocks in a chilled Collins or highball glass.

2 oz. gin

1 oz. cherry brandy or Peter Heering

Juice of $\frac{1}{2}$ lemon

Dash of Benedictine

In a shaker with cracked ice combine all ingredients except for lemon slice and mint sprig, but including a splash of club soda. Shake vigorously. Strain into the serving glass. Add ice cubes and club soda to fill. Garnish with lemon slice and mint sprig.

Pink Lady

Serve straight up in a chilled cocktail glass.

3 oz. gin

2 tsp. sugar syrup

3 oz. applejack or Calvados

2 tsp. grenadine

2 oz. lemon juice

1 egg white*

Combine all ingredients, with ice, in a shaker. Shake vigorously. Strain into serving glasses. Recipe makes two drinks.

* *Raw egg may be a source of salmonella bacteria. You may wish to avoid drinks calling for raw egg yolk or egg white.*

Diamond Head

Serve straight up in a chilled cocktail glass.

1¹/₂ oz. gin

¹/₂ oz. curaçao

2 oz. pineapple juice

1 tsp. sweet vermouth

In a shaker or blender, mix all ingredients with cracked ice. Strain into serving glass.

Na Zdorovye!
The World of Vodka

In This Chapter

- Vodka comes to America
- Almost flavorless and wildly flavorful
- The Bloody Mary—history and recipes
- Favorite vodka recipes

Colorless, tasteless, and aromaless, vodka outsells any other category of spirits in the United States. This may strike you as surprising when you consider that vodka was rarely consumed here before World War II. During the war, Americans were subjected to rigorous rationing of almost every product, including booze. Peace brought an end to rationing, but, after four years of war, liquor dealers had precious little product to offer. That's when the thirsty discovered a small distillery with a proud Russian name, Smirnoff, which had been making vodka since the end of Prohibition. With a hole to fill in the market, Smirnoff grew, and soon America was served by a bevy of domestic and foreign vodka distillers.

Squeaky Clean

By U.S. law, all nonflavored vodka consumed here must be filtered after distillation to remove all distinctive character, aroma, taste, and color. However, even the flavorless vodkas—especially the premium brands—do have a certain character, an undertone of flavor, which partisans of particular brands prize. Shop—and sip—around.

And also take notice of the rainbow of flavored—yes, *flavored*—vodkas that have appeared in recent years. Infusions of peppercorns, lemon peel, raisins, anise, basil, berries (especially black currant), and caraway are especially popular.

Bloody Mary: A Multifaceted Classic

Now, some folks just throw a little vodka and a little tomato juice together and hand you what they call a Bloody Mary. But that's, at best, a vodka and tomato juice, not a Bloody Mary. The classic recipe, evolved and elaborated upon from Harry's original, follows.

 Bar Tips _____

Most shaker drinks should be shaken vigorously, but not the Bloody Mary. Shake *too* hard, and the tomato juice may separate. Go gently.

Bloody Mary

Serve in a chilled Collins glass.

2 oz. Vodka

4–6 oz. tomato juice

1 tsp. lemon juice

$1/4$ tsp. Worcestershire sauce

Few dashes Tabasco sauce

Pinch white pepper

Pinch or two of celery salt

$1/2$ tsp. dried or fresh chopped dill

Celery stalk

Combine all ingredients (except for the celery stalk) with cracked ice in a shaker. Shake gently. Pour into the serving glass. Garnish with celery stalk and, if you wish, add two or three ice cubes.

Here are two variations on the classic:

Bloody Blossom

Serve in a Collins glass.

$1^1/2$ oz. vodka

3 oz. orange juice

3 oz. tomato juice

Mint sprig

In a shaker, combine all ingredients except mint sprig with cracked ice. Shake gently. Pour into the serving glass, and garnish with mint.

Ginza Mary

Serve in a chilled old-fashioned glass.

1¹/₂ oz. vodka

1¹/₂ oz. tomato juice or V-8

1¹/₂ oz. sake

¹/₂ oz. lemon juice

Few dashes Tabasco

Few dashes soy sauce

Pinch white pepper

Combine all ingredients in a mixing glass. Stir, and then pour into serving glass.

From the Citrus Grove

Vodka mixes beautifully with citrus juices. Don't invest in premium-label vodka for citrus drinks; instead, spend a little extra to buy freshly-squeezed juices or spend a little extra time to squeeze the juice fresh yourself. You'll taste the difference.

Cape Codder

Serve in a large (double) chilled old-fashioned glass.

1¹/₂ oz. vodka	4 oz. cranberry juice
Dash lime juice	1 tsp. sugar syrup

Combine all ingredients in a shaker with cracked ice. Shake vigorously, and pour into the serving glass.

Vodka Gimlet with Fresh Lime

Serve on the rocks in a lowball glass.

2 oz. vodka

1 oz. fresh lime juice

Combine ingredients in a shaker. Shake vigorously. Pour into the serving glass. Or, combine both ingredients in the serving glass and stir.

Vodka Gimlet with Rose's Lime Juice

Serve in a chilled cocktail glass.

2 oz. vodka

$1/2$ oz. Rose's lime juice

Combine both ingredients with ice in a mixing glass. Stir. Strain into the serving glass.

Cayman Cup

Serve in a chilled Collins glass.

$1^1/2$ oz. vodka

$1/2$ oz. triple sec

2 oz. mango nectar

2 oz. orange juice

$1/2$ oz. lemon juice

Mango and/or peach slices

In a shaker or blender combine all ingredients except fruit slices. Blend or shake with cracked ice, and then pour into serving glass. Garnish with fruit slices.

Driving a Screw and Banging a Wall

To think of vodka and orange juice is to think of a screwdriver, a very basic drink named for a very basic tool. It's best if the orange juice is freshly squeezed!

Screwdriver

Serve on the rocks in a chilled highball glass or in a large (double) chilled old-fashioned glass.

1¹/₂ oz. vodka

4 oz. orange juice

Orange slice

Fill serving glass one third with ice cubes. Pour in vodka and orange juice, stir, and garnish with orange slice.

The Harvey Wallbanger is a step beyond a screwdriver, and the other drinks in this section take a leap or two beyond that.

Harvey Wallbanger

Serve on the rocks in a chilled Collins glass.

1¹/₂ oz. vodka

4 oz. orange juice

¹/₂ oz. Galliano

Fill serving glass one third with ice cubes. Pour in vodka and orange juice, and stir. Carefully add the Galliano so that it floats. Do not stir!

Fuzzy Navel

Serve on the rocks in a highball glass.

³/₄ oz. peach schnapps

³/₄ oz. vodka

Orange juice to fill

Combine all ingredients in the serving glass and stir.

Original Sex on the Beach

Serve in a chilled highball glass.

1 oz. vodka

¹/₂ oz. Midori melon liqueur

¹/₂ oz. Chambord (substitute other raspberry liqueur if necessary)

1¹/₂ oz. pineapple juice

1¹/₂ oz. cranberry juice cocktail

Combine all ingredients in a shaker with ice. Shake vigorously and pour into the serving glass.

Alternative Sex on the Beach

Serve on the rocks in a highball glass.

³/₄ oz. peach schnapps

³/₄ oz. vodka

3 oz. pineapple or grapefruit juice

3 oz. cranberry juice cocktail

Combine all ingredients in the serving glass with ice and stir.

A shooter is meant to be downed in a single swallow, attended by a rush of pleasurable pain. The Kamikaze is one of the most, shall we say, acute. Banzai!

Kamikaze

Serve in three shot glasses.

1 oz. vodka

1 oz. triple sec

1 oz. lime juice

Combine ingredients in a shaker, and shake with ice; then strain into *three* shot glasses.

The Russians Are Coming

Here are three "Russian"—i.e., vodka—classics every bartender should know.

Black Russian

Serve in a chilled old-fashioned glass.

$1^1/_2$ oz. vodka

$^3/_4$ oz. Kahlua

Combine the two ingredients with cracked ice in a shaker. Shake vigorously, and then pour into the serving glass. Optionally, add a few dashes of lemon juice for a "Black Magic." Garnish with lemon twist, if desired.

White Russian

Serve in a chilled cocktail glass.

1¹/₂ oz. vodka

1 oz. white crème de cacao

³/₄ oz. heavy cream

Combine the ingredients with cracked ice in a shaker. Shake vigorously, and then strain into the serving glass.

Russian Coffee

Serve in a chilled brandy snifter.

¹/₂ oz. vodka

1¹/₂ oz. coffee liqueur

1 oz. heavy cream

Combine all ingredients in a blender with ice. Blend until smooth, and then pour into the snifter.

Bar Tips

Vodka is becoming increasingly popular as an alternative to gin in martinis, but don't look for your vodka martini here. You'll find it, with its gin-based brethren, in Chapter 5.

The Vodka ...

Be inventive. The range of possible vodka combinations is limited only by your imagination.

Vodka Collins

Serve on the rocks in a Collins glass.

1 oz. vodka

2 oz. sour mix

Club soda to fill

Maraschino cherry

Combine all ingredients except for cherry in the serving glass filled with ice. Stir. Garnish with cherry.

Bar Tips

If you don't want to use store-bought sour mix, see Chapter 1 for a fresh homemade recipe.

Vodka Cooler (Simple)

Serve on the rocks in a Collins glass.

1 oz. vodka

$^1/_2$ oz. sweet vermouth

7-Up to fill

Combine vodka and sweet vermouth in a shaker with ice. Shake vigorously. Strain into serving glass filled with ice. Add 7-Up to fill.

Vodka Grasshopper

Serve in a chilled cocktail glass.

$1/2$ oz. vodka

$3/4$ oz. green crème de menthe

$3/4$ oz. white crème de menthe

Combine the ingredients with cracked ice in a shaker. Shake vigorously, and then strain into the serving glass.

Jungle Jim

Serve in a chilled old-fashioned or lowball glass.

1 oz. vodka

1 oz. crème de banane

1 oz. milk

Combine all the ingredients with cracked ice in a shaker. Shake vigorously, and then pour into the serving glass.

Vodka Sour

Serve straight up in a chilled sour glass.

$1 1/2$–2 oz. vodka   Lemon slice

$3/4$ oz. lemon juice   Maraschino cherry

1 tsp. sugar syrup

Combine all ingredients except lemon slice and cherry in a shaker with cracked ice. Shake vigorously. Strain into the serving glass and garnish with lemon slice and maraschino cherry.

Vodka Stinger

Serve in a chilled cocktail glass.

1¹/₂ oz. vodka

1 oz. white crème de menthe

Combine all ingredients in a shaker with cracked ice. Shake vigorously and strain into the serving glass.

Vodka Tonic

Serve on the rocks in a highball glass.

1¹/₂ oz. vodka

Tonic water to fill

Lime wedge

Pour vodka into a serving glass one-third full of ice. Add tonic to fill, and garnish with lime wedge.

Vodka is a neutral spirit you can mix with almost anything. If you need a little help, see Appendix B for more ways to quench your thirst.

The Silver Bullet Reloaded

In This Chapter

- Secrets and controversies
- How dry is a dry martini?
- The basic martini
- Martini nouveau

Even though the classic "three-martini lunch" has diminished in popularity since the IRS reduced the allowable deduction on business entertaining, the martini remains at once the most sophisticated, variable, refined, controversial, popular, and—yes—innovative of cocktails. Self-proclaimed purists have a lot to say about how a martini should be made, and that includes forbidding vodka as an ingredient. "You can make a very nice drink with vodka and vermouth," they say, "but it's not a martini."

This chapter aims to please the purists, but it also covers not only the vodka martini but some recent innovations on the martini concept.

> **Buzzed Words** _____
>
> A **dry martini** is one with relatively little vermouth versus gin. Some drinkers prefer 12 parts gin to 1 part vermouth, while others insist on a 20-to-1 ratio. Extremists do away with the vermouth altogether and have a gin and olive on the rocks.

Martini Secrets

Here are the 10 secrets of making a great martini:

1. For a gin martini, use a premium-label gin. Which one you use is up to you. They range in degree of flavorfulness. If you like a martini redolent of aromatic botanicals, veer toward the Bombay end of the gin spectrum. If you prefer a cleaner taste, lean toward Beefeater. Something in between? Taste Tanqueray. Try them all in your favorite club, and then bring home your favorite.

2. For a vodka martini, use a premium-label vodka. The variations in flavorfulness and character among these are less pronounced than among premium-label gins, but you may want to sample several to find a favorite.

3. Use a dry vermouth that you would enjoy drinking by itself, on the rocks. Two brands, Noilly-Prat and Martini and Rossi, dominate the market. Both are excellent. Sample and decide.

4. Use super-clean glassware for mixing as well as for serving. Make certain there is no detergent or soap aftertaste.

5. Whether you serve your martini straight up or on the rocks, use ice that is entirely free from freezer burn or freezer-borne smells and tastes. Commercial bagged ice is always best.

6. Never use olives stuffed with pimento. They will discolor the drink and give it an unwanted flavor.

7. But … never say never. Some martini lovers like pimento in their olive and don't mind the drink's pinkish hue and peppery flavor one bit.

8. If you are the host, *listen* to the drinker. Based on your taste and experience, you may suggest this or that ratio and this or that gin, but don't force anything on anyone. Accommodate the drinker.

9. Don't let *anyone* tell you there's only one "right" way to make a martini.

10. But it's not worth fighting over. Give peace a chance.

The Classic Dry Martini

We believe that the "dry" martini is the closest thing there is to a "standard" martini. Here's how it's done.

**Quick One** _____

An Air Force pilot always packed gin
and vermouth, olives, a mixing spoon, and a
chrome-plated cup. One day, his copilot
asked, "What good will all that do if we
crash in the jungle?" The pilot answered,
"We go down in the middle of nowhere, I
start making a martini, and somebody will
show up and say, '*That's* no way to make a
martini!'"

Dry Martini

Serve in a chilled cocktail glass.

2 oz. gin

¹/₂ tsp. dry vermouth

Olive or lemon twist

Combine gin and vermouth in a mixing glass at
least half full of ice. Stir well, and then strain
into the cocktail glass. Garnish with olive or
lemon twist. If your olives are very small, spear
three on a toothpick.

Quick One _____

"Let me slip out of these wet clothes
and into a dry martini."
—Robert Benchley, Algonquin wit

If you want to taste more of the vermouth, make the martini less dry by adding more vermouth. Many drinkers favor a 5-to-1 ratio.

A dry vodka martini should be drier than the dry gin martini. Here's a starting point most drinkers will enjoy.

Dry Vodka Martini

Serve in a chilled cocktail glass.

3 oz. vodka

Dash of dry vermouth

Olive or lemon twist

Combine vodka and vermouth in a mixing glass at least half full of ice. Stir well, and then *quickly* strain into the cocktail glass. Garnish with olive or lemon twist. If your olives are very small, spear three on a toothpick.

Bar Tips _____

Both the gin and vodka martinis—but especially the vodka martini—benefit from quick stirring with a lot of ice rather than prolonged stirring with a few ice cubes. The object is to minimize meltage, which dilutes the drink. One of the few things martini drinkers agree on is that a watery drink stinks.

But wait—there's the *perfect* martini, and then there's the *Perfect* Martini. The presumptuous name comes from the exquisite yin and yang of the sweet versus the dry vermouth.

Perfect Martini

Serve in a chilled cocktail glass.

1^1/$_2$ oz. gin

^{1}/$_2$ tsp. dry vermouth

^{1}/$_2$ tsp. sweet vermouth

Olive

Combine all ingredients except olive in a mixing glass with ice. Stir well and strain into the serving glass. Garnish with olive.

The Really Dry Martini

There are at least three ways to make a *really* dry martini:

- Using the same amount of gin or vodka as for the basic dry martini, add just two or three *drops* of vermouth. No, you don't need an eye dropper. Just put your thumb over the mouth of the bottle and sprinkle.

- Pour an ounce or so of dry vermouth into a chilled cocktail glass. Swirl the vermouth to coat the glass. Pour out the excess vermouth. Stir the gin or vodka in a mixing glass with ice. Strain into the coated cocktail glass.

- Forget the vermouth altogether. Serve straight gin or vodka on the rocks or straight up (having stirred the spirit with ice). Call it a really dry martini (but it's really just cold gin).

Gibson

The Gibson is the most common variation on the martini theme. At its most basic, it's just a martini with a few (three or more, depending on size and preference) pickled pearl onions instead of the olive or lemon twist. The conscientious Gibson maker, however, varies the underlying martini recipe slightly, yielding a somewhat larger drink that is *always* on the very dry side.

The Vodka Gibson is almost identical to the Gin Gibson. Just add a bit more vodka.

Gibson

Serve in a chilled cocktail glass.

2½ oz. gin

Dash or two of dry vermouth

Pickled pearl onions

Combine gin and vermouth in a mixing glass at least half full of ice. Stir well, and then *quickly* strain into the cocktail glass. Garnish with pearl onions.

Bar Tips

Take a moment to blot the pickled pearl onions with a paper towel. This will remove excess vinegar, which might otherwise give an unwanted flavor to the drink.

Bar Tips

Glasses stored for a long time in a closed cabinet sometimes acquire a musty, dusty taste. Rinse out even clean glasses if they have been stored for any length of time.

Vodka Gibson

Serve in a chilled cocktail glass.

3 oz. vodka

Dash or two of dry vermouth

Pickled pearl onions

Combine vodka and vermouth in a mixing glass at least half full of ice. Stir well, and then *quickly* strain into the cocktail glass. Garnish with pearl onions.

 Bar Tips

To chill a glass, fill it with ice, add water, and let it sit while you mix the drink. When ready to pour, dump the water and ice, shake the glass to remove the excess, and pour the drink!

Two Vodka Variations

Blue Sky Martini

Serve straight up in a chilled cocktail glass.

2$\frac{1}{2}$ oz. Skyy Vodka

$\frac{1}{2}$ oz. Blue Curaçao

Lemon twist

Combine in a shaker with cracked ice. Shake, and strain into the serving glass. Garnish with lemon twist.

Flirtini

Serve straight up in a chilled cocktail glass.

$\frac{1}{2}$ oz. Stolichnaya Razberi Vodka

$\frac{1}{2}$ oz. Cointreau

Splash lime juice

Splash pineapple juice

Splash cranberry juice

Brut champagne

Few raspberries

Mint sprig

Muddle (mash and stir) raspberries in bottom of a cocktail glass. Combine the first five ingredients in a shaker with cracked ice. Shake, and then strain into the cocktail glass. Add brut champagne to fill, and garnish with sprig of mint.

Not Your Father's Martini

By now we've either reeducated (fat chance!) or thoroughly alienated the martini purists out there, so let's plunge ahead boldly into the depths of decadence with a catalogue of martini exotica.

Chocolate Martini

Serve in a martini glass.

2 oz. vodka

$^1/_2$ oz. crème de cacao

Combine both ingredients in a shaker filled with ice. Pour into the serving glass.

Hawaiian Martini

Serve in a chilled cocktail glass.

$1^1/_2$ oz. gin

1 tsp. dry vermouth

1 tsp. sweet vermouth

1 tsp. pineapple juice

Combine all ingredients in a shaker with ice. Shake well, and strain into the serving glass.

Orgasm Martini

Serve in a martini glass.

1^1/$_2$ oz. vodka

Splash Triple Sec

Splash white crème de cacao

Orange slice

Combine all ingredients except orange slice in a shaker with cracked ice. Shake, and then strain into serving glass. Garnish with orange slice.

Rum Martini

Serve in a chilled cocktail glass.

2 oz. white rum

Several drops of dry vermouth

Olive

Lime twist

Combine the ingredients except olive and lime twist in a mixing glass with ice. Stir well and strain into the serving glass. Garnish with olive and lime twist.

The Tequini doffs a sombrero to the country south of the border. It's a martini made with tequila instead of gin.

Tequini

Serve in a chilled cocktail glass.

2^1/$_2$ oz. tequila

^{1}/$_2$ oz. dry vermouth

Olive or lemon twist

Combine all ingredients except olive or lemon twist in a mixing glass with ice. Stir well and strain into the serving glass. Garnish with olive or lemon twist.

Lemon Drop

Serve in a chilled cocktail glass.

2 oz. Absolut Citron

Lemon wedge, sugared

Pour vodka into mixing glass with ice. Swirl or stir, and then strain into serving glass. Garnish with sugared lemon wedge.

Slippery Knob

Serve in a chilled cocktail glass.

1^1/$_2$ oz. gin

Splash Grand Marnier

Combine ingredients in a shaker or mixing glass. Shake or stir with cracked ice, and then strain into the serving glass.

The martini may be approached with religious purity or with a wanton appetite for adventure and invention. Either way, stop arguing about the "perfect" martini and just mix up whatever variation you enjoy.

Chapter 6

Mostly Bourbon (and a Touch of Tennessee)

In This Chapter

- Bourbon vs. Tennessee whiskey
- How to enjoy whiskey neat
- Bourbon and whiskey recipes

"The United States is the world's largest producer and consumer of whiskey," the *Encyclopedia Britannica*'s article on "whiskey" concludes matter-of-factly. But the numbers are anything but matter of fact: Americans have more than *500 brands* of the great American whiskey, bourbon, to choose from. How many other products can you think of that are offered in 500 brands?

Nor is there any product more American than bourbon. It is rooted in colonial times and was among the very first of American industries. It was also among the first products the Feds hit on as a source of tax revenue—something that led George Washington to call out the militia against Pennsylvania moonshiners during the Whiskey Rebellion of 1794.

This chapter will tell you what all the fuss has been about for all these years.

Neat, Rocks, Branch, Soda

Really good whiskey is a pleasure to enjoy neat (straight, no ice, no water), on the rocks, with club soda, or with what southerners (and those with a hankering to sound like southerners) like to call *branch* or *branch water*, which, these days, is plain old tap water.

Bar Tips

The cowpoke thrusts aside the swinging saloon doors, moseys up to the bar, orders a shot of whiskey, and downs it in a gulp. You can do this, too. But why waste *really good* whiskey? Fine whiskey, like fine wine, is meant to be savored and is best enjoyed slowly.

What do you need to know about enjoying whiskey unadorned? A little ...

- Invest in a premium-label bourbon or Tennessee whiskey. With some 500 brands, you have a lot of sampling to do.
- Generally speaking, higher-proof whiskies are best for sipping.
- Use scrupulously clean and thoroughly rinsed glassware.
- Use ice that is free from freezer burn and freezer odors and tastes. Commercial bagged ice is often best.

- If your tap water tastes good, use it. Otherwise, consider bottled spring water. If you are *really* serious about sampling a variety of whiskies, use distilled water, which is the most neutral mixer available.

- If you want effervescence, you can mix your whiskey with club soda, soda water, seltzer, or even unflavored sparkling water, such as Perrier, which, however, will impart a slight mineral taste. If you want the most neutral carbonated mixer, use soda water.

Juleps: Some Schools of Thought

Among the most delightful—and potent—of bourbon mixed drinks is the julep. Just as the subject of the martini sparks debate in the chilly north, so, in the sunny south, the julep is a source of arcane disputation. Here are three juleps that claim to be "standard."

Mint Julep Version 1

Serve in an old-fashioned glass.

$^1/_2$ tsp. fine-grained sugar

$2^1/_2$ oz. bourbon

Splash club soda

Mint sprig

Put the $^1/_2$ teaspoon of sugar in the bottom of the mixing glass. Fill the glass one-third full with ice cubes. Add bourbon. Add splash of club soda. Garnish with mint sprig.

Mint Julep 2

Serve in a Collins glass.

2 oz. bourbon

6 mint leaves

$^{1}/_{2}$ oz. sugar syrup

Mint sprig

Place mint leaves in the bottom of the serving glass and add sugar syrup. Mash leaves in syrup. Add half the bourbon, and then fill the glass with crushed ice. Add the balance of the bourbon and stir vigorously. Garnish with mint sprig.

Mint Julep 3

Serve in an old-fashioned or Collins glass.

1 cube sugar

3 oz. bourbon

Mint sprigs

Dissolve sugar cube in the bottom of the serving glass with a few drops of plain water. Add a few mint sprigs. Fill the glass with ice (cubes or crushed), and then add bourbon. Stir well. Cut up some more mint sprigs and add these to the drink. Stir, and then allow to stand several minutes before serving.

The Frozen Julep departs, quite bracingly, from the standard—whatever *that* is.

Frozen Julep

Serve in a large (double) old-fashioned glass.

2 oz. bourbon

1 oz. lemon juice

1 oz. sugar syrup

6 small mint leaves

Mint sprig

In a mixing glass, muddle mint leaves together with bourbon, lemon juice, and sugar syrup. Put muddled ingredients in a blender with crushed ice. Blend until ice becomes mushy. Pour into the serving glass and garnish with mint sprig.

Buzzed Words _____

To **muddle** is to mash and stir. Mint leaves and other solids are muddled in order to make a suspension or a paste with fluid. A special pestle-like wooden **muddler** can be used to muddle, but any spoon will do.

Some Classic Bourbon and Tennessee Cocktails

Tennessee whiskey is produced in Kentucky's neighbor, Tennessee, from sour mash, which mixes new mash (the fermentable mixture from which whiskey is made) with old mash from the previous batch of whiskey.

A mellow corn note distinguishes the flavor of Tennessee whisky from that of bourbon, but, in the classic recipes that follow, you can use bourbon or Tennessee whiskey interchangeably. Of course, you owe it to yourself to try sipping a fine Tennessee whisky (such as Jack Daniel's, George Dickel, or Evan Williams) straight—just to see for yourself that, while interchangeable as mixers, bourbon and Tennessee whiskey are distinctive in themselves.

Bluegrass Cocktail

Serve in a chilled cocktail glass.

1½ oz. Bourbon or Tennessee whiskey

1 oz. pineapple juice

1 oz. lemon juice

1 tsp. maraschino liqueur

Combine all ingredients in a shaker with ice. Shake vigorously, and then strain into the serving glass.

Strictly speaking, a *cobbler* is an iced drink made with wine or liqueur plus sugar and fruit juice; however, no one is likely to complain if you throw in some bourbon. Beware. Like the Mint Julep, this is a potent blend. Sugar and carbonated water speed the absorption of alcohol into the bloodstream. The drink goes down so easily that you and your guests will be tempted to gulp. Sip! Please!

Bourbon Cobbler

Serve in a chilled highball glass.

1½ oz. bourbon or Tennessee whiskey

1 tsp. sugar syrup

1 oz. Southern Comfort

1 tsp. peach-flavored brandy

2 tsp. lemon juice

Club soda to fill

Peach slice

Combine all ingredients except club soda and peach slice in a shaker with cracked ice. Shake vigorously, and then pour into serving glass. Add several ice cubes, and then club soda to fill. Garnish with peach slice.

Made with the traditional gin, it's called a Tom Collins. With bourbon, some call it a John Collins—a nod, doubtless, to the spirit of John Barleycorn, traditional personification of alcohol. You can have yours relatively subdued or jet-assisted, with higher-proof bourbon and a Peychaud's send-off.

Bourbon Collins (Unadorned)

Serve in a chilled Collins glass.

1 oz. bourbon or Tennessee whiskey

$^1/_2$ oz. lime juice

1 tsp. sugar syrup

Club soda to fill

Lime peel

Combine all ingredients except lime peel and club soda in a shaker with cracked ice. Shake vigorously, and then pour into the serving glass. Add club soda to fill and garnish with lime peel.

Bourbon Collins (Augmented)

Serve in a chilled highball glass.

2 oz. 100-proof bourbon or Tennessee whiskey

$^1/_2$ oz. lemon juice

1 tsp. sugar syrup

Few dashes of Peychaud's bitters

Club soda to fill

Lemon slice

Combine all ingredients except lemon slice and club soda in a shaker with cracked ice. Shake vigorously, and then pour into the serving glass. Add club soda to fill and garnish with lemon slice.

Bourbon Manhattan

Serve in a chilled cocktail glass.

2 oz. bourbon or Tennessee whiskey

$^1/_2$ oz. sweet vermouth

Dash Angostura or other bitters

Maraschino cherry

Combine all ingredients except cherry in a mixing glass with ice. Stir well, and then strain into the serving glass. Garnish with cherry.

Bourbon Old-Fashioned

Serve on the rocks in an old-fashioned glass.

$1^1/_2$ oz. bourbon or Tennessee whiskey

Splash of water

Dash sugar syrup

Liberal dash Angostura bitters

Combine all ingredients over ice in the serving glass. Stir well.

Bourbon Rose (Dark)

Serve in a chilled highball glass.

1¹/₂ oz. bourbon or Tennessee whiskey

4 oz. orange juice

1 oz. triple sec

Grenadine

Combine all ingredients except grenadine in a shaker with cracked ice. Shake vigorously, and then pour into the serving glass. *Carefully* pour a float of grenadine on top. Do not stir.

Bourbon Rose (Pale)

Serve in a chilled old-fashioned glass.

1¹/₂ oz. bourbon or Tennessee whiskey

¹/₂ oz. dry vermouth

¹/₂ oz. crème de cassis

¹/₂ oz. lemon juice

Combine all ingredients in a shaker with cracked ice. Shake vigorously, and then pour into the serving glass.

Bourbon Sidecar

Serve in a chilled cocktail glass.

1½ oz. bourbon or Tennessee whiskey

¾ oz. curaçao or triple sec

½ oz. lemon juice

Combine all ingredients in a shaker with cracked ice. Shake vigorously, and then strain into the serving glass.

Fontainebleau Sidecar

Serve in a chilled wine goblet.

2 oz. bourbon or Tennessee whiskey

1 oz. curaçao (may substitute Cointreau)

Juice of ½ lemon

Grand Marnier

Combine all ingredients except for Grand Marnier in a shaker or blender with cracked ice. Shake or blend, and then pour into serving glass. Float one or two teaspoons of Grand Marnier on top. Do *not* stir!

Bourbon Sour

Serve in a chilled Sour glass.

2 oz. bourbon or Tennessee whiskey

Juice of $1/2$ lemon

$1/2$ tsp. sugar syrup

Maraschino cherry

Orange slice

Combine all ingredients except fruit in a shaker with ice. Shake vigorously, and then strain into the serving glass. Garnish with fruit.

Retuning the Old Boy Network

Bourbon has a not entirely undeserved reputation as a man's drink—or, more precisely, an "old boy's drink." It summons up visions of darkly paneled club rooms thick with cigar smoke. Let's clear the air and shake it up. It is a fact that most committed bourbon drinkers shy away from scotch (and vice versa), but they usually enjoy gin well enough. Hence the Dry Mahoney.

Dry Mahoney

Serve in a chilled cocktail glass.

$2\frac{1}{2}$ oz. bourbon

$\frac{1}{2}$ oz. dry vermouth

Lemon twist

Combine all ingredients except lemon twist in a mixing glass filled with ice. Stir vigorously, and then strain into the serving glass. Garnish with lemon twist. It is recommended that the drink be served with a few ice cubes on the side, in a second glass.

Old money, new, or very little of either, here is an almost achingly rich cocktail.

Millionaire Cocktail

Serve in chilled cocktail glasses.

3 oz. bourbon

1 oz. Pernod

Few dashes curaçao

Few dashes grenadine

1 egg white*

Combine all ingredients in a mixing glass with cracked ice. Stir well, and strain into the serving glasses. *Recipe makes two drinks.*

* *Raw egg may be a source of salmonella bacteria. You may wish to avoid drinks calling for raw egg yolk or egg white.*

Bar Tips _____

Most drinks that call for egg whites require half an egg white. But it's almost impossible to get *half* an egg white; therefore, all recipes in this book calling for egg white make *two* drinks.

What's the origin of the name of the following drink? We have so far failed to discern the religious significance of combining ginger ale with club soda. Still, it's a pretty good drink.

Presbyterian

Serve on the rocks in a highball glass.

3 oz. bourbon

Equal portions of ginger ale and club soda to fill

Pour bourbon into serving glass half filled with ice cubes. Add equal portions of ginger ale and club soda to fill.

Ward Eight

Serve in a chilled cocktail glass.

2 oz. bourbon

1 oz. lemon juice

1 oz. orange juice

Sugar syrup to taste

Dash grenadine

Combine all ingredients in a shaker with ice. Shake vigorously and strain into the serving glass.

Two New Orleans Legends

Go down to New Orleans, and you'll find the Sazerac in high demand and plentiful supply.

Simple Sazerac

Serve in a chilled old-fashioned glass.

$1/4$ tsp. Pernod or other absinthe substitute

$1/2$ tsp. sugar

1 TB. water

Dash Peychaud's bitters

2 oz. bourbon (may also use rye or blended whiskey)

Lemon peel

Coat the serving glass by swirling Pernod in it. Add sugar, water, and Peychaud's. Muddle these until sugar is completely dissolved. Add bourbon with a few ice cubes. Stir vigorously. Garnish with lemon peel.

Next, the "Original Sazerac"—at least, almost. Originally, the drink contained a hearty dose of absinthe, a powerful extract of wormwood. Because of its nasty knack for inducing hallucinations, convulsions, and general mental debility, absinthe was outlawed in the States and many other countries. Never fear. Herbsaint is an absinthe stand-in that may be hard to find outside of New Orleans; however, you may substitute with Pernod.

Buzzed Words

Absinthe is an aromatic, bitter, very strong liqueur flavored chiefly with wormwood and other botanicals. Absinthe was outlawed in many countries early in the twentieth century because of its apparent toxicity.

Original Sazerac

Serve in a chilled old-fashioned glass.

1 sugar cube

2 dashes Peychaud's bitters

Dash Angostura bitters

2 oz. 100-proof bourbon (may substitute rye or blended whiskey)

Dash Herbsaint (may substitute with Pernod)

Lemon peel

Use crushed ice to chill *two* old-fashioned glasses. Pour out ice from one glass. In the bottom of that glass put sugar cube with a few drops of water. Add bitters, and muddle sugar and bitters until sugar is dissolved. Add bourbon and ice cubes. Stir well. Empty the second glass of ice and add a liberal dash of Herbsaint, swirling to coat the glass. Discard excess bitters and pour in mixture from first glass. Twist lemon peel over the glass, but *do not garnish with lemon peel;* discard.

If you're a bourbon drinker, give Tennessee whiskey a chance. And if Dickel or Jack is your whiskey of choice, why not sample a bourbon now and then?

Chapter 7

Blends of Canada and the Lower Forty-Eight

In This Chapter

- How blended whiskey is made
- Why blended whiskey is a great mixer
- How to select a blended whiskey
- Blended whiskey recipes

Most Americans enjoy lighter beverages than Europeans drink; for example, in the United States, ale and stout have never been as popular as beer. So it is with whiskey. To be sure, many Americans like their bourbon and scotch, but blended whiskey is a North American phenomenon, a beverage that is less filling and lighter in body than bourbon, Tennessee whiskey, scotch, or rye. Some of the most popular U.S. and Canadian whiskies are blended. They make great mixers, as you'll see.

Alcoholic Alchemy

Blended whiskies may combine various straight whiskies (whiskies distilled from the mash of a single grain) only, or may involve combinations of *straight whiskies*, *mixed-grain whiskies*, grain neutral spirits, and so-called *light whiskies*. The latter are whiskies distilled at high proof—over 160—and stored in used charred oak barrels. The result is more flavorful than neutral spirits, but not as strong as straight whiskey. In a blend, light whiskey imparts character without compromising the light, dry quality desired in a blend.

The creation of a fine blended whiskey is as much art as a science. It is a kind of alchemy, presided over by a *master blender*, who may combine as many as 50 whiskies drawn from a "library" of hundreds of products.

Buzzed Words

Straight whiskey is made from mash containing at least 51 percent of a certain grain; however, straight corn whiskey mash contains 80-percent corn. With **mixed-grain whiskies**, no single grain predominates. **Light whiskey** is distilled in excess of 160 proof and aged in charred oak barrels. An important component in blended whiskey, it is more flavorful than neutral spirits, but not as strong as straight whiskey.

W-H-I-S-K-Y: Savoring the Canadian Difference

Canadian whisky is so light, they even take the *e* from between the *k* and *y* to spell it. Very light, delicately flavored, and exceedingly smooth, Canadian whisky makes for an ideal mixer.

Neat, Rocks, Soda, Ginger

You'll want to devote a good deal of pleasurable effort to discovering your favorite blends, particularly if you intend to enjoy the whiskey neat, on the rocks, or with plain soda. But beware! Soapy glasses, chlorine-laden tap water, or freezer-burned ice will really wreck the taste of delicately flavored American and Canadian blends.

Ginger ale has always been a popular mixer with blended whiskey. Just pour a jigger of whiskey into a highball glass filled with ice and add ginger ale to fill. If you want something a little fancier and quite a bit stronger, try the Horse's Neck.

Horse's Neck

Serve in a chilled Collins glass.

1 lemon

2–3 oz. blended whiskey

Ginger ale

Chill a Collins glass, drop in a long lemon-peel strip, add whiskey and ice cubes, and then a few drops of lemon juice. Fill with ginger ale and stir very gently.

You'll Take Manhattan

The woodwind tones of a good blended or Canadian whisky are perfectly suited to the Manhattan. Made with care, the Manhattan is a delicate and subtle drink, despite its essential sweetness. While many people have theirs on the rocks, it is best enjoyed well chilled, straight up. The basic, unadorned recipe follows—and then some variations.

Manhattan

Serve in a chilled cocktail glass.

2 oz. blended whiskey   Dash Angostura bitters

1/2 oz. sweet vermouth   Maraschino cherry

Combine all ingredients except cherry with ice in a mixing glass. Stir well, and then strain into the serving glass and garnish with cherry.

Dry Manhattan

Serve in a chilled cocktail glass.

2 oz. blended whiskey

1/2 oz. dry vermouth

Dash Angostura bitters (optional)

Lemon twist

Combine all ingredients except lemon twist with ice in a mixing glass. Stir well, and then strain into the serving glass and garnish with lemon twist.

Old-Fashioned Manhattan

Serve in a chilled cocktail glass.

1¹/₂ oz. blended whiskey

1¹/₂ oz. sweet vermouth

Maraschino cherry

Combine ingredients except cherry in a shaker with cracked ice. Shake vigorously, and then pour into the serving glass and garnish with cherry.

Perfect Manhattan

Serve in a chilled cocktail glass.

2 oz. blended whiskey

¹/₂ oz. sweet vermouth

¹/₄ oz. dry vermouth

Dash Angostura bitters

Maraschino cherry

Combine all ingredients except cherry in a mixing glass with ice. Stir well, and then strain into the serving glass and garnish with cherry.

Biscayne Manhattan

Serve in a chilled cocktail glass.

1 ¹/₂ oz. blended whiskey

¹/₂ oz. sweet vermouth

2 oz. orange juice

Few dashes yellow Chartreuse

Orange slice

In a shaker or blender, combine all ingredients except for orange slice. Shake or blend, and then strain into serving glass. Garnish with orange slice.

Bar Tips _____

You can make the recipes in this chapter with American or Canadian blended whiskey; however, at the end of the chapter you'll find a group of recipes in which the ultra-light Canadian product works best.

Listen to it Fizz

Blended whiskey is the perfect choice for fizz drinks because its light qualities complement effervescence and don't fight sweet mixers.

Whiskey Curacao Fizz

Serve in a chilled Collins glass.

2 oz. blended whiskey   1 tsp. sugar

½ oz. curacao   Club soda to fill

1 oz. lemon juice   Orange slice

Combine all ingredients except orange slice and club soda in a shaker with cracked ice. Shake well, and then pour into the serving glass. You may add additional ice cubes, if you wish. Add club soda to fill. Garnish with orange slice.

Whiskey Fizz

Serve in a chilled highball glass.

1½ oz. blended whiskey

½ tsp. sugar syrup

Few dashes Angostura bitters

Club soda to fill

Combine all ingredients except club soda in the serving glass one-third full of ice. Stir well, and then add club soda to fill.

Peel Me a Grapefruit

While the combination of bourbon or scotch with grapefruit juice may appall some, the cleaner, lighter taste of blended whiskey makes the combination seem perfectly natural.

Grapefruit Cooler

Serve in a chilled Collins glass.

2 oz. blended whiskey

4 oz. grapefruit juice

$1/2$ oz. red currant syrup

$1/4$ oz. lemon juice

$1/2$ orange slice

$1/2$ lemon slice

Combine all ingredients except fruit in a shaker with cracked ice. Pour into the serving glass, adding ice cubes, if you wish. Garnish with orange and lemon.

De Rigueur

Serve in a chilled cocktail glass.

$1^1/2$ oz. blended whiskey

$1/2$ oz. grapefruit juice

2 tsp. honey

In a shaker or blender, combine all ingredients with cracked ice. Shake or blend, and then strain into serving glass.

Old-Fashioneds and a Rickey

Some folks say that only bourbon makes a *real* old-fashioned, and it can't be denied that bourbon gives the drink added body. But substituting Canadian or other blended whiskey introduces a lighter note for a kinder, gentler drink.

Then there's the rickey. A *gin* drink, yes? Well, usually. But the light taste of Canadian or other blended whiskey is not as far from the feel of gin as you may at first think.

Blended Whiskey Old-Fashioned

Serve on the rocks in an old-fashioned glass.

1$^{1}/_{2}$ oz. blended whiskey

Dash water

Dash sugar syrup

Liberal dash Angostura bitters

Combine all ingredients in a serving glass half full of ice.

Canadian Old-Fashioned

Serve in a chilled old-fashioned glass.

1$^{1}/_{2}$ oz. Canadian whisky

$^{1}/_{2}$ tsp. curaçao

Dash lemon juice

Dash Angostura bitters

Lemon twist

Orange twist

Combine all ingredients except twists in a shaker with cracked ice. Shake vigorously, and then pour into the serving glass. Garnish with twists.

Whiskey Rickey

Serve on the rocks in a Collins glass.

1$\frac{1}{2}$ oz. blended whiskey

Juice of $\frac{1}{2}$ lime

1 tsp. sugar syrup

Club soda to fill

Lime twist

Combine all ingredients except lime twist and club soda in the serving glass at least half filled with ice. Stir well. Add club soda to fill and garnish with lime twist.

Pucker Up!

The name aside, a whiskey sour should be both sweet and sour, evoking both a pucker and a smile.

Whiskey Sour

Serve in a chilled sour glass.

2 oz. blended whiskey

1 oz. sour mix

Maraschino cherry

Orange slice

Combine all ingredients except fruit in a shaker with cracked ice. Shake vigorously. Pour into the serving glass and garnish with fruit.

Alternative Whiskey Sour

Serve in a chilled sour glass.

2 oz. blended whiskey	Maraschino cherry
1 oz. lemon juice	Orange slice
1 TB. sugar syrup	

Combine all ingredients except fruit in a shaker with cracked ice. Shake vigorously. Pour into the serving glass and garnish with fruit.

How Sweet It Is

Blended whiskey takes remarkably well to a little sweetness and light.

New Yorker

Serve in a chilled cocktail glass.

1½ oz. blended whiskey	Dash grenadine
½ oz. lime juice	Lemon twist
1 tsp. sugar syrup	Orange twist

Combine all ingredients except fruit in a shaker with ice. Shake vigorously, and then pour into the serving glass and garnish with twists.

Buzzed Words

A **daisy** is a whiskey- or gin-based drink that includes some sweet syrup and a float of (usually golden) liqueur.

Candy Pants

Serve in a chilled cocktail glass.

1¹/₂ oz. blended whisky

¹/₂ oz. cherry-flavored brandy

1 tsp. lemon juice

Sugar syrup (to taste)

Dash grenadine

In a shaker or blender combine all ingredients with cracked ice. Shake or blend, and then strain into serving glass.

Peachtree Street

Serve in a chilled cocktail glass.

1¹/₂ oz. blended whiskey

1 oz. Southern Comfort

Few dashes orange bitters

Maraschino cherry

In a shaker or blender, combine all ingredients, except for cherry, with cracked ice. Shake or blend, and then strain into serving glass. Garnish with cherry.

Toast

May you live forever, and may I never die.

7&7

Serve on the rocks in a highball glass.

1¹/₂ oz. Seagram's 7-Crown

4 oz. 7-Up

Pour whiskey into the serving glass filled with ice. Add 7-Up.

Mixing Whiskey with Wine— and Liqueur

What's the old saying? "Beer and whiskey, kind of risky. Whiskey and wine, tastes fine." Pretty tempting combined with the right liqueur, too.

Ladies' Cocktail

Serve in a chilled cocktail glass.

1¹/₂ oz. blended whiskey

1 tsp. anisette

Few dashes Pernod

Few dashes Angostura bitters

Pineapple stick

Combine all ingredients except pineapple stick in a shaker with cracked ice. Shake vigorously and strain into the serving glass. Garnish with pineapple stick.

Madeira Cocktail

Serve in a chilled old-fashioned glass.

1¹/₂ oz. blended whiskey

1¹/₂ oz. Malmsey Madeira

1 tsp. grenadine

Dash lemon juice

Orange slice

Combine all ingredients except orange slice in a shaker with cracked ice. Shake vigorously and pour into the serving glass. Garnish with orange slice.

O, Canada!

All of the recipes in this chapter can be made with Canadian whisky instead of American blended whiskey, if you prefer. But here are a few drinks *especially* for Canadian whisky. Its very light taste makes these work.

Dog Sled

Serve in a chilled old-fashioned glass.

2 oz. Canadian whisky

2 oz. orange juice

1 TB. lemon juice

1 tsp. grenadine

Combine all ingredients with cracked ice in a shaker. Shake vigorously, and then pour into the serving glass.

Frontenac Cocktail

Serve in a chilled cocktail glass.

1¹/₂ oz. Canadian whisky

¹/₂ oz. Grand Marnier

Few dashes kirsch

Dash orange bitters

Combine all ingredients with cracked ice in a shaker. Shake vigorously, and then pour into the serving glass.

Saskatoon Stinger

Serve on the rocks in an old-fashioned glass.

2 oz. Canadian whisky

1 oz. peppermint schnapps (may substitute white crème de menthe)

Lemon twist

Pour whisky and schnapps into the serving glass half filled with ice cubes. Stir well, and garnish with lemon twist.

With their light body, blended whiskey and Canadian whisky can often go where no bourbon has gone before: in a great variety of sweet and delicately flavored mixed drinks.

Chapter **8**

Comin' Through the Rye

In This Chapter

- Why rye is a "drinker's drink"
- Where rye comes from
- A good reason to avoid cheap rye
- Rye recipes

Rye is one of those spirits people call a "drinker's drink," which means that a lot of folks just don't like the stuff. It does come on strong, but if you like scotch, rye is worth giving a chance. This chapter has some suggestions for enjoying this black sheep among whiskies.

Baa, Baa Black Sheep

Rye is a cereal grain that has been cultivated at least since 6500 B.C.E. Despite its pedigree, it's always been something of a second-class grain, grown mainly where the climate and soil are unsuited to other, more favored cereals, or cultivated as a winter crop in places too cold to grow winter wheat. You can make a loaf of bread with rye, but, even here, it doesn't measure up to wheat because it lacks the requisite elasticity. The rye bread most of us eat is almost always a blend of rye and wheat. Traditionally, black bread, made entirely from rye, has been associated with poverty. So, there it is: the rather sad story of this hearty, but hard-pressed cereal grain. And it gets sadder. While pumpernickel bread, made from rye, has become somewhat more popular in recent years, rye whiskey, in many places, has all but disappeared.

Bar Tips

Rye has fallen so far out of the loop that drinkers who ask for "rye and ginger" are probably expecting to be served a blended whiskey with ginger ale. Respond to the request as thus—"Do you want rye or blended whiskey?"

Rye, Buck Naked

The fact is, rye offers a full-bodied, up-and-at-'em alternative to scotch and Irish whiskey, the two whiskey types it most resembles in flavor. Just be sure to invest in a good rye. Cheap brands give new meaning to the term *rotgut* and are characterized by a musty taste—like sipping something that's been sitting in a damp basement for far too long. Drinking rye should not be a punishment. In many liquor stores, you'll find but a single premium brand,

Old Overholt, the most widely marketed rye. Fortunately, it's quite good.

Rock and Rye: What It Is and What You Can Do with It

Rock and rye is not rye whiskey on the rocks. It is a liqueur, marketed under various brand names, made with rye whiskey, whole fruits—you'll actually see them in the bottle—and rock candy. Since every time you say "rye in a crowd," the phrase "rock and rye" will jump up like a leg whose knee has been tapped by a rubber mallet, you'd better know what to do with rock and rye.

Basically, there are two things you can do. You can make a *cooler* or you can make a *heater*—better known as a toddy.

Rock and Rye Cooler

Serve in a highball glass.

1½ oz. vodka

1 oz. rock and rye

2 tsp. lime juice

Lemon-lime soda to fill

Lime slice

Combine all ingredients except soda in a shaker with ice. Shake vigorously, and then strain into the serving glass half filled with ice cubes. Add lemon-lime soda to fill and garnish with lime slice.

Rock and Rye Toddy

Serve in a heat-proof mug.

2 oz. rock and rye

2 dashes Angostura bitters

Lemon slice

3 oz. boiling water

Cinnamon stick

Grated nutmeg

Combine rock and rye with bitters in the mug. Drop in lemon slice, and then pour on boiling water. Garnish with cinnamon stick and grated nutmeg.

Certain old-timers swear by the Rock and Rye Toddy as a sovereign cure for the common cold. Cure? Not likely. Comfort? Perhaps.

Buzzed Words

A **toddy** is a hot drink consisting of liquor (often rum), water, sugar, and spices.

To Fizz or to Flip?

A *fizz* is just about any drink made with sugar and soda, and a *flip* is a drink with liquor, sugar, spice, and egg. Both have pleasantly old-fashioned qualities, which make them the perfect haven for rye, itself an old-fashioned spirit.

Rye Fizz

Serve on the rocks in a highball glass.

1½ oz. rye   Dash sugar syrup

Dash Angostura bitters   Club soda to fill

Combine all ingredients except soda in a mixing
glass. Stir well and pour into the serving glass
filled with ice. Add club soda to fill.

Bar Tips

The best way to chill a brandy snifter is
with crushed ice. Pour it into the snifter, allow
the snifter to chill, and then pour out the ice
when you are ready to pour in the drink.
Putting a delicate snifter in a refrigerator or
freezer may crack it.

Rye Flip

Serve in a chilled brandy snifter.

1½ oz. rye   1 tsp. sugar syrup

1 egg *   Ground nutmeg

Combine all ingredients except nutmeg in a
shaker with ice. Shake vigorously, and then
strain into the serving glass. Sprinkle with
nutmeg.

* *Raw egg may be a source of salmonella bacteria. You may wish
to avoid drinks calling for raw egg yolk or egg white.*

The Pick-Me-Ups

Some call these fortifiers, others, pick-me-ups. Whatever you call them, they make an impression and leave a glow.

Old Pepper

Serve in a whiskey sour glass or wine goblet.

1½ oz. blended whiskey

¾ oz. rye

1 oz. lemon juice

Dash Worcestershire sauce

Dash chili sauce

Dash Tabasco

2 dashes Angostura bitters

Combine ingredients in a shaker with plenty of cracked ice. Shake, and then pour into serving glass. No need to strain out the ice.

Hunter's Cocktail

Serve on the rocks in an old-fashioned glass.

1½ oz. rye

½ oz. cherry brandy

Maraschino cherry

Combine rye and brandy over ice in the serving glass. Stir, and then garnish with cherry.

Yashmak

Serve in a chilled highball glass.

³/₄ oz. rye

³/₄ oz. dry vermouth

1 TB. Pernod

Dash Angostura bitters

3–4 drops of sugar syrup

In a shaker combine all ingredients with cracked ice. Shake vigorously, and then strain into serving glass. Add ice cubes to taste.

Citrus Sensations

Bal Harbour is a Florida coastal community so upscale that it had to spell its name the British way. Its namesake cocktail smacks of easy living among old money.

Bal Harbour Cocktail

Serve in a chilled cocktail glass.

1¹/₂ oz. rye

¹/₂ oz. dry vermouth

1 oz. grapefruit juice

Maraschino cherry

Combine all ingredients except cherry in a shaker with cracked ice. Shake vigorously, and then strain into the serving glass. Garnish with maraschino cherry.

Rye Showcases

Rye really comes into its own when combined with liqueurs and bitters. These drinks are decidedly not for people who want a "lite" experience. They'll take you the whole nine yards.

Frisco Cocktail

Serve in a chilled cocktail glass.

1¹/₂ oz. rye

1¹/₂ oz. Benedictine

¹/₂ oz. lemon juice

Orange twist

Combine all ingredients except orange twist in a shaker with ice. Shake vigorously, and then strain into the serving glass and garnish with twist.

Lord Baltimore's Cup

Serve in a chilled large wine glass or wine goblet.

¹/₂ tsp. sugar syrup

Few dashes Angostura bitters

1 oz. rye

Champagne to fill

1 tsp. Pernod for float

Combine sugar and bitters in the serving glass. Add rye, along with several ice cubes, and then fill with champagne. Carefully add Pernod as a float. Do not stir.

Ten Ton Cocktail

Serve in a chilled cocktail glass.

1 1/2 oz. rye

1 TB. dry vermouth

1 TB. grapefruit juice

Cherry

Combine all ingredients except cherry in a shaker with cracked ice. Shake, and then strain into serving glass. Garnish with cherry.

Rye Comes to Manhattan

The versatile Manhattan can be made with bourbon, blended whiskey, scotch, and rye. The basic recipe follows.

Rye Manhattan

Serve in a chilled cocktail glass.

1 1/2 oz. rye

1/4 oz. sweet vermouth

Maraschino cherry

Combine rye and vermouth in a mixing glass filled with ice. Stir well, and then strain into the serving glass and garnish with cherry.

Dry Rye Manhattan

Serve in a chilled cocktail glass.

1¹/₂ oz. rye

¹/₄ oz. dry vermouth

Maraschino cherry

Combine rye and vermouth in a mixing glass filled with ice. Stir well, and then strain into the serving glass and garnish with cherry.

Perfect Rye Manhattan

Serve in a chilled cocktail glass.

2 oz. rye

¹/₂ tsp. sweet vermouth

¹/₂ tsp. dry vermouth

Few dashes Agnostura bitters

Maraschino cherry

Combine all ingredients except cherry in a shaker with ice. Shake vigorously, and then strain into the serving glass and garnish with cherry.

Quick One

Commuter to train conductor: "This morning I accidentally left a small bottle of rye on the train. Was it turned into the Lost-and-Found?"

"No," the conductor replied, "but the guy who found it was."

Two For the Road

Before you leave this chapter, check out this pair of particularly provocative rye mixers.

The Devil

Serve in a chilled cocktail glass.

1 oz. rye whiskey

1 oz. orange juice

Grenadine

1 maraschino cherry

Combine rye and orange juice in a shaker with cracked ice. Shake, and then strain into serving glass. Drizzle grenadine and garnish with cherry.

Indian River Rye Cocktail

Serve in a chilled old-fashioned glass.

1 oz. rye	2 oz. orange juice
1 oz. dry vermouth	Few dashes raspberry syrup

Combine all ingredients in a shaker with cracked ice. Shake vigorously, and then pour into the serving glass.

Toast

Here's to you and here's to me. And here's to love and laughter. I'll be true as long as you. But not a minute after.

Chapter 9

Spirits of Thistle and Shamrock

In This Chapter

- Scotch connoisseurship
- Irish whiskey: a comer
- Single malt vs. blends
- Scotch recipes

Like fine wine, scotch has long been popular in America, but, as with wine, recent years have seen a popular upsurge in the connoisseurship of scotch, especially the single malts.

Again, as with wine, creating scotch is theoretically quite simple. There is fermentation, distilling, aging, and then bottling. In the case of blended scotch, there is the added complication of blending 15 to 50 whiskies. Yet, still, as the saying goes, this isn't rocket science. Nevertheless, scotch varies greatly in taste from label to label, and just why this is the case is a subject of deep mystery and lively debate.

As for Irish whiskey, its legion of admirers is smaller than the host who clamor for scotch, but, thanks in part to the great popularity of a number of liqueurs based on Irish whiskey (paramountly Irish Mist and Bailey's Original Irish Cream), the whiskey itself is enjoying increasing demand in the United States.

Single Malt vs. Blended

The casual scotch drinker may or may not be familiar with the distinction between *malt* and grain whiskies, but all except the absolute neophyte have heard something about single-malt versus blended scotches.

Buzzed Words _____

Malt is grain (usually barley) that has been allowed to sprout.

Despite the effort that goes into creating blended scotch, it is much less expensive than single-malt scotch, which currently accounts for a scant 2 percent of scotch sales. As the name implies, single-malt scotch is made exclusively from malted barley, which means that it is aged at least 14 years. Moreover, the whiskey in a bottle of single-malt scotch has been distilled and aged during a single continuous period and by a single distillery.

Premium blended scotches can be very fine indeed, but a good single malt is a work of very patient art, with a range of flavor as subtle and varied as that of superb vintage wine. The best-known names among the malted scotches ring out with Celtic grandeur: The Glenlivet, Knockando, Glenfiddich, Laphroaig, Glenmorangie, and Macallan. There is, of course, the matter of price: high.

Buzzed Words

Malt scotches are made entirely from malted barley and are distilled in relatively small pot stills. **Grain scotches** combine malted barley with unmalted barley and corn and are distilled in "continuous" stills.

Pleasure Unalloyed: Neat, Rocks, Water, Soda

For the lover of fine scotch, few gustatorial pleasures exceed that of sampling the many blended and single-malt varieties available. Any of the premium-priced blended labels make for enjoyment, especially served on the rocks or with a plain mixer. The single-malt scotches are best-enjoyed neat—and absolutely *any* of these is sure to delight. Irish whiskey is likewise rewarding neat or on the rocks. Just remember the rules of enjoying fine whiskey in its unadorned state:

- Use super-clean glassware that is free from soap and detergent residue.
- Make certain any water that you add has no unwanted flavors or odors.

- Use the best ice possible. If you must take it from your freezer, run some water over it to get rid of freezer burn and any stray odors or flavors.

Scotch: The Classic Menu

If you plan on mixing your scotch with something more than ice or water, it's a good idea to review some of the classic combinations. The Rob Roy is among the most frequently requested.

Rob Roy

Serve in a chilled cocktail glass.

2 oz. scotch

$\frac{1}{2}$ oz. sweet vermouth

Maraschino cherry

Combine scotch and sweet vermouth in a mixing glass with ice. Stir well, and then strain into the serving glass and garnish with cherry. For a Dry Rob Roy, substitute dry vermouth and garnish with a lemon twist. You'll find a variation in Appendix B.

This simple combination of scotch and scotch liqueur is among the most popular of scotch-based mixed drinks.

Toast

Women have many faults, but men have only two: everything they say and everything they do!

Highland Fling with Milk

Serve in a chilled old-fashioned glass.

1 1/2 oz. scotch

3 oz. milk

1 tsp. sugar syrup

Ground nutmeg

Combine all ingredients except nutmeg in a shaker with cracked ice. Shake vigorously, and then pour into the serving glass and sprinkle with nutmeg.

Highland Fling with Sweet Vermouth

Serve in a chilled cocktail glass.

1 1/2 oz. scotch

1/2 oz. sweet vermouth

Few dashes orange bitters

Olive

Combine all ingredients except olive in a shaker with cracked ice. Shake vigorously, and then strain into the serving glass and garnish with olive.

HAHAH Quick One _____

> Two men meet in a sleazy dockside bar.
>
> "Lemme tell ya. It's gotten to the point where I get drunk mostly on water."
>
> "That's crazy," the other man said. "Impossible!"
>
> "It's a fact. Especially when you're cooped up with nothin' but men on the ship."

Spiritual Unions

Scotch marries well with liqueurs, especially Drambuie, Scotland's immensely popular scotch-based liqueur.

Rusty Nail

Serve on the rocks in an old-fashioned glass.

1½ oz. scotch

1 oz. Drambuie

Combine ingredients in the serving glass half filled with ice cubes. Stir. (If you prefer, the Drambuie can be floated without stirring.)

The Godfather

Serve in a chilled old-fashioned glass.

1½ oz. scotch

¾ oz. Amaretto di Saronno

Combine with several ice cubes in the serving glass.

Bar Tips

For mixed drinks, use blended scotch. There is no sane reason to expend the precious nectar of single-malt scotch in combination with strongly flavored mixers.

Blackwatch

Serve on the rocks in a highball glass.

1$\frac{1}{2}$ oz. scotch   Lemon slice

$\frac{1}{2}$ oz. curaçao   Mint sprig

$\frac{1}{2}$ oz. brandy

Combine all ingredients except lemon slice and mint sprig in the serving glass half filled with ice cubes. Stir gently, and then garnish with lemon slice and mint sprig.

Colloden Cheer

Serve in a chilled cocktail glass.

1 oz. scotch

1 oz. dry sherry

$\frac{1}{2}$ oz. lemon juice

$\frac{1}{2}$ oz. La Grande Passion

In a shaker or blender combine all ingredients. Shake or blend. Strain into the serving glass.

The Sweeter Side

Scotch is naturally the sweetest of whiskies and takes well to the more sugary mixers.

Inverness Cocktail

Serve in a chilled cocktail glass.

2 oz. scotch

$1/2$ oz. lemon juice

1 tsp. orgeat syrup

1 tsp. curaçao (may substitute triple sec)

Combine all ingredients except for curaçao in a shaker or blender with cracked ice. Strain into serving glass. Float curaçao on top. Do not stir!

Smashes are drinks with loads of crushed ice.

Scotch Smash

Serve in a large (double) old-fashioned glass.

6 mint leaves

Heather honey (may substitute sugar syrup)

3 oz. scotch

Orange bitters

Muddle (mash and stir) honey (or sugar syrup) with mint leaves in the serving glass, and then fill the glass with finely crushed ice. Add scotch and stir well. Dash on a topping of orange bitters and garnish with mint sprig.

With Versatile Vermouth

Vermouth is not just for gin and vodka. You'll need sweet as well as dry for these scotch and vermouth combinations.

Blood and Sand

Serve in a chilled old-fashioned glass.

$^3/_4$ oz. scotch

$^3/_4$ oz. cherry brandy

$^3/_4$ oz. sweet vermouth

$^3/_4$ oz. orange juice

Combine all ingredients in a shaker with cracked ice. Shake vigorously, and then pour into the serving glass.

Bobby Burns

Serve in a chilled cocktail glass.

$1^1/_2$ oz. scotch

$^1/_2$ oz. dry vermouth

$^1/_2$ oz. sweet vermouth

Dash Benedictine

Combine all ingredients in a shaker with ice. Shake vigorously, then strain into the serving glass.

Brigadoon

Serve in a chilled old-fashioned glass.

1 oz. scotch

1 oz. grapefruit juice

1 oz. dry vermouth

Combine all ingredients in a shaker with cracked ice. Shake vigorously, and then pour into the serving glass.

The Irish Are Coming

The fine, thin note of Irish whiskey never over-powers whatever it's mixed with; therefore, make sure you mix it only with very good things.

Blackthorn

Serve in a chilled old-fashioned glass.

1½ oz. Irish whiskey

1½ oz. dry vermouth

Liberal dashes Pernod

Liberal dashes Angostura bitters

Combine all ingredients in a shaker with cracked ice. Shake vigorously and pour into the serving glass.

Cocktail Na Mara ("Cocktail of the Sea")

Serve in a chilled highball glass.

2 oz. Irish whiskey

2 oz. clam juice

4 oz. tomato juice

$^1/_2$ oz. lemon juice

Few dashes Worcestershire sauce

Dash Tabasco sauce

Pinch white pepper

Into a mixing glass combine all ingredients. Stir well with cracked ice, and then pour into serving glass.

Irish Rainbow

Serve in a chilled old-fashioned glass.

$1^1/_2$ oz. Irish whiskey

Liberal dashes Pernod

Liberal dashes curaçao

Liberal dashes maraschino liqueur

Liberal dashes Angostura bitters

Orange twist

Combine all ingredients except twist in a shaker with cracked ice. Shake vigorously, and then pour into the serving glass. Garnish with orange twist.

The Mists of Eire

Irish Mist is a highly popular and readily available liqueur based on Irish whiskey. Combined with more of its mother ingredient, it makes for some tempting whiskey-and-liqueur libations.

Ballylickey Belt

Serve in an old-fashioned glass.

$^1/_2$ tsp. heather honey   Club soda to fill

$1^1/_2$ oz. Irish whiskey   Lemon twist

Dissolve honey with a few splashes of club soda in the bottom of the serving glass. Add whiskey and a few ice cubes, and then club soda to fill. Garnish with twist.

Irish Fix

Serve in a chilled old-fashioned glass.

2 oz. Irish whiskey

$^1/_2$ oz. Irish Mist

$^1/_2$ oz. lemon juice

$^1/_2$ oz. pineapple syrup (may substitute pineapple juice sweetened with a little sugar)

Orange slice

Lemon slice

Combine all ingredients except fruit in a shaker with cracked ice. Shake vigorously, and then pour into the serving glass. Garnish with the fruit slices.

A Sweet Bouquet

Irish whiskey is the first choice for these, but feel free to substitute a blended scotch, if you like.

Bow Street Special

Serve in a chilled cocktail glass.

1½ oz. Irish whiskey

¾ oz. triple sec

1 oz. lemon juice

Combine the ingredients in a shaker with cracked ice. Shake vigorously, and then pour into the serving glass.

Grafton Street Sour

Serve in a chilled cocktail glass.

1½ oz. Irish whiskey

½ oz. triple sec

1 oz. lime juice

¼ oz. raspberry liqueur

Combine all ingredients except raspberry liqueur in a shaker with ice. Shake vigorously, and then strain into the serving glass. Carefully top with liqueur.

Paddy Cocktail

Serve in a chilled cocktail glass.

1 1/2 oz. Irish whiskey

3/4 oz. sweet vermouth

Liberal dashes Angostura bitters

Combine the ingredients in a shaker with cracked ice. Shake vigorously, and then pour into the serving glass.

Wicklow Cooler

Serve in a chilled Collins glass.

1 1/2 oz. Irish whiskey

1 oz. dark Jamaica rum

1/2 oz. lime juice

1 oz. orange juice

1 tsp. orgeat syrup

Ginger ale

Combine all ingredients except ginger ale in a shaker or blender with cracked ice. Shake or blend, and then pour into serving glass. Add a few ice cubes, if desired. Top off with ginger ale.

Resist the temptation to buy any old scotch or Irish whiskey and settle on it. That's like buying a bottle of burgundy and making that your "red" forever. Play the field. Sample the variety.

Chapter 10

Caribbean Sugar: A Rum Resumé

In This Chapter

- Rum—a spirit of great variety
- The distinctive character of rums from different countries
- Straight or mixed
- Rum recipes

To think of rum only as a clear, sweet liquor to mix with a Coke or to throw into a daiquiri is to ignore a whole dazzling tropical and semitropical world. The fact is, even drinkers who are sophisticated in the nuances of bourbon and Tennessee whiskey and blended versus single-malt scotches often know very little about rum. It is produced in a vast variety of flavors in countries spanning the Caribbean and the Atlantic coast of Central and South America.

So Near and Yet So Far

As with most spirits, the basic process of making rum is simple. Most rums are made from molasses, the residue that remains after sugar has been crystallized from sugarcane juice.

It is significant that the sugar necessary for fermentation is present in the molasses, which means that, more than any other distilled spirit, rum retains the flavor of the raw material from which it is made. This accounts in large part for the great variation in flavor and character among rums produced in different regions.

Another determinant of taste and character is the type of yeast employed to trigger the fermentation process. Each producer of rum closely guards its unique strain of yeast. Finally, distillation methods, aging duration and conditions, and blending also contribute to distinctive flavor. As with the blending of whiskey, the blending of rum is the work of a master blender who tests, chooses, and combines the products of various distilleries and various ages to achieve a rum of distinctive character and consistent quality.

Rum and Nada

Most people think of rum as a mixer, period. But the truly great rums also deserve to be sampled straight, sipped like fine wine or good whiskey. To do so can become a cruise through the Caribbean and the coasts of Central and South America.

In general, the characteristic rums of Jamaica and the Demerara River region of Guyana are dark, heavy, and sweet. Barbados rums are golden or dark amber and neither as heavy nor as sweet as those of Jamaica or Demerara. Today, the characteristic rums of Puerto Rico and the Virgin Islands follow the pattern set by Bacardi in the mid-nineteenth century in that they are dry and light. Long-aged rums—some of the best of which are produced in Colombia (Ron Medellin) and Venezuela (Cacique Ron Anejo)—take on a rich golden-amber color from the American Oak barrels in which they are stored for as much as 10 years.

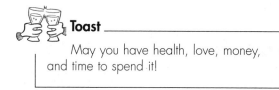

Toast

May you have health, love, money, and time to spend it!

Bacardis

In the world of rum, Bacardi is the most familiar brand name. It is also the name of one of the most frequently requested rum drinks. Two versions follow.

Bacardi

Serve in a chilled cocktail glass.

1½ oz. light or gold Bacardi rum

½ oz. lime juice

½ tsp. grenadine

Combine all ingredients in a shaker with cracked ice. Shake vigorously, and then pour into the serving glass.

Bacardi Special

Serve in a chilled cocktail glass.

1 1/2 oz. light Bacardi rum

3/4 oz. gin

1/2 oz. lime juice

1/2 tsp. grenadine

Combine all ingredients in a shaker with cracked ice. Shake vigorously, and then pour into the serving glass.

Cuba Libre!

The fancy name for a rum and Coke is a Cuba Libre. Want a lower-calorie drink? Use diet cola.

Cuba Libre

Serve on the rocks in a highball glass.

1 1/2 oz. light or gold rum

Coca-Cola or other cola soft drink to fill

Lime wedge

Combine all ingredients except lime in the serving glass filled with ice. Garnish with lime wedge.

If you want to transform this familiar drink into something special, use dark rum and some cherry brandy, plus cola.

Cherry Cola

Serve on the rocks in a lowball glass.

2 oz. dark rum

$^1/_2$ oz. cherry brandy

2 oz. Coca-Cola or other cola soft drink to fill

Lemon twist

Combine the ingredients in the serving glass filled with ice. Garnish with twist.

A Pair of Coladas

Piña coladas are delicious coconut, pineapple juice, and rum drinks. Here are two of the tastiest.

Piña Colada with Light Rum

Serve in a chilled Collins glass.

1$^1/_2$ oz. light rum	Splash cream
1 oz. cream of coconut	Maraschino cherry
2 oz. canned pineapple chunks	Orange slice
	Pineapple stick
2 oz. pineapple juice	

Combine all ingredients except fruit in a blender with 3 ounces of crushed ice. Blend until smooth, and then pour into the serving glass and garnish with fruit.

Piña Colada with Gold Rum

Serve in a chilled Collins glass.

2 oz. gold rum

2 oz. cream of coconut

4 oz. pineapple juice

Pineapple stick

Maraschino cherry

Combine all ingredients except fruit in a shaker with crushed ice. Shake vigorously, and then pour into the serving glass. Garnish with fruit.

Daiquiri Dimensions

The traditional daiquiri is sweetened with sugar. Ernest Hemingway's favorite drink, when he was game fishing in Cuba, was an unsugared daiquiri. Of course, his favorite sandwich consisted of nothing but raw onions between bread.

Buzzed Words

A **daiquiri** is a rum, lime juice, and sugar drink named after the Cuban town near the original Bacardi rum distillery.

Daiquiri

Serve in a chilled cocktail glass.

2 oz. light rum

Juice of $^1/_2$ lime

$^1/_2$ tsp. sugar syrup

Orange slice

Combine all ingredients except orange slice
in a shaker with ice. Shake vigorously, and then
strain into the serving glass.

Daiquiri Dark

Serve in a chilled Collins glass.

2 oz. Jamaican rum

$^1/_2$ oz. lime juice

$^1/_2$ tsp. sugar syrup

Combine all ingredients in a shaker with ice.
Shake vigorously, and then strain into the serving glass.

Bar Tips

Exotic rum drinks are best served in fun
vessels—the kitschier the better. Comb flea
markets and second-hand stores for Hurricane glasses, totem cups, and the like.
Freely substitute these for the glassware recommended in this chapter.

Banana Daiquiri

Serve in a chilled cocktail glass.

1½ oz. light rum   1 tsp. sugar syrup

½ oz. lime juice   ½ ripe banana, sliced

Combine all ingredients in a blender with cracked ice. Blend until smooth, and then pour into the serving glass.

Strawberry Daiquiri

Serve in a chilled cocktail glass.

1½ oz. light rum

½ oz. lime juice

1 tsp. sugar syrup

6 large strawberries (fresh or frozen)

Combine all ingredients in a blender with cracked ice. Blend until smooth, and then pour into the serving glass.

Peach Daiquiri

Serve in a chilled cocktail or wine glass.

2 oz. light rum   1 tsp. sugar syrup

½ oz. lime juice   ½ oz. peach juice

Combine all ingredients in a blender with cracked ice. Blend until smooth, and then pour into the serving glass.

Citrus Combinations

Rum loves the company of citrus juices—and, if taste in any indication, the juices freely reciprocate the good feelings.

Javier Saavedra

Serve in a chilled cocktail glass.

1 oz. dark Jamaican rum

1 oz. white tequila

2 oz. pineapple juice

1 oz. grapefruit juice

Orange slice

Combine all ingredients except orange slice in a shaker or blender with cracked ice. Shake or blend, and then strain into serving glass. Garnish with orange slice.

Buzzed Words

Grog was originally nothing more than rum diluted with water and rationed to sailors of the eighteenth-century Royal Navy. Its namesake was Admiral Edward Vernon (1684–1757), who first ordered the ration: Vernon's nickname was Old Grogram, after his habit of wearing a grogram (coarse wool) cloak.

Navy Grog

Serve in a chilled large (double) old-fashioned glass.

1 oz. light rum

1 oz. dark Jamaican rum

1 oz. 86-proof Demerara rum

$1/2$ oz. orange juice

$1/2$ oz. guava juice

$1/2$ oz. lime juice

$1/2$ oz. pineapple juice

$1/2$ oz. orgeat syrup

Lime slice

Mint sprig

Combine all ingredients except lime slice and mint sprig in a shaker with cracked ice. Shake vigorously, and then pour into the serving glass and garnish with lime slice and mint sprig.

Zombie

Serve in a chilled Collins glass.

2 oz. light rum

1 oz. dark Jamaican rum

$1/2$ oz. 151-proof Demerara rum

1 oz. curaçao

1 tsp. Pernod

1 oz. lemon juice

1 oz. orange juice

1 oz. pineapple juice

$1/2$ oz. papaya juice

$1/4$ oz. grenadine

$1/2$ oz. orgeat syrup

Mint sprig

Pineapple stick

Combine all ingredients except pineapple stick and mint sprig in a blender with 3 ounces cracked ice. Blend until smooth, and then pour into the serving glass and garnish with mint sprig and pineapple stick.

Island Hopping

The following is a round-up of some of the most popular rum-based tropical concoctions. Each is an instant vacation in paradise.

Blue Hawaiian

Serve in a chilled Collins glass.

2 oz. light rum

1 oz. blue curaçao

1 oz. sour mix

1 oz. orange juice

1 oz. pineapple juice

Combine all ingredients in a blender with 3 ounces cracked ice. Blend until smooth, and then pour into the serving glass.

Hurricane

Serve in a chilled cocktail glass.

1 oz. light rum

1 oz. gold rum

$\frac{1}{2}$ oz. passion fruit syrup

$\frac{1}{2}$ oz. lime juice

Combine all ingredients in a shaker with ice. Shake vigorously, and then strain into the serving glass.

Little Dix Mix

Serve in a chilled old-fashioned glass.

1½ oz. dark Jamaican rum

½ oz. crème de banane

½ oz. lime juice

1 tsp. curaçao

Combine all ingredients with cracked ice in a shaker or blender. Shake or blend. Pour into serving glass.

 Toast _____

All that we have drunk, sung, and danced, no one will ever take away from us.

Mai Tai

Serve in a chilled old-fashioned glass.

1 oz. Jamaican rum	¼ oz. orgeat syrup
1 oz. Martinique rum	Lime twist
½ oz. curaçao	Mint sprig
¼ oz. rock-candy syrup	Pineapple stick

Combine all ingredients except twist, sprig, and stick in a shaker with cracked ice. Shake vigorously, and then pour into the serving glass and garnish with the lime, mint, and pineapple.

With Liqueur and Brandy

Watch out for these! The combination of rum and liqueur is seductive as well as potent. Too much of these good things will create the mother of all hangovers.

Between the Sheets

Serve in a chilled cocktail glass.

³/₄ oz. light rum

³/₄ oz. brandy

³/₄ oz. Cointreau

¹/₂ oz. lemon juice

Combine all ingredients with ice in a shaker. Shake vigorously, and then strain into the serving glass.

Outrigger

Serve in a chilled cocktail glass.

1 oz. gold rum

1 oz. brandy

1 oz. triple sec

¹/₂ oz. lime juice

Combine all ingredients in a shaker with ice. Shake vigorously, and then strain into the serving glass.

Tiger's Milk

Serve in a chilled wine goblet.

1^1/$_2$ oz. Bacardi Añejo gold rum

Sugar syrup to taste

1^1/$_2$ oz. cognac

4 oz. half-and-half

Grated nutmeg

Combine all ingredients except nutmeg in a shaker with cracked ice. Shake vigorously, and then pour into the serving glass. Dust with grated nutmeg.

A One-Two Planter's Punch

Planter's Punch is claimed as the property of the folks who make Myers's Rum. This is the recipe you'll find on a bottle of their dark rum.

The *Plantation* Punch throws Southern Comfort and brown sugar into the mix.

Planter's Punch

Serve in a chilled Collins glass.

2 oz. Myers's dark rum	Dash grenadine
3 oz. orange juice	Orange slice
Juice of ^{1}/$_2$ lemon or lime	Maraschino cherry
1 tsp. sugar	

Combine all ingredients except fruit in a shaker with cracked ice. Shake vigorously, and then pour into the serving glass. Garnish with orange slice and maraschino cherry.

Plantation Punch

Serve in a chilled Collins glass.

1¹/₂ oz. dark Jamaican rum	Club soda to fill
³/₄ oz. Southern Comfort	Orange slice
1 tsp. brown sugar	Lemon slice
1 oz. lemon juice	1 tsp. port

Combine all ingredients except club soda, fruit, and port in a shaker with cracked ice. Shake vigorously, and then pour into the serving glass. Add club soda to fill and garnish with fruit. Top off with port.

Toast

To love and laughter and happily ever after!

Rum and Joe

Jamaican Coffee is also called a Calypso, and it makes a splendid after-dinner drink.

Jamaican Coffee (a.k.a. Calypso)

Serve in a coffee mug.

³/₄ oz. Tia Maria	Hot coffee
³/₄ oz. Jamaican rum	Whipped cream

Pour Tia Maria and rum into the mug and add coffee. Top with whipped cream.

Café Foster

1 oz. light or dark rum

$^1/_2$ oz. crème de banana

Hot coffee

Whipped cream

Pour rum and crème de banana into mug. Add coffee to fill, and then top with whipped cream.

In addition to the many original mixed drinks featuring rum, the tropical spirit can stand in for a variety of liquors in familiar drinks. See Appendix B for all the rum variations of classics like the martini, the Collins, and the screwdriver.

Chapter 11

Tequila!

In This Chapter

- The truth about tequila
- How tequila is made
- Tequila in white and gold
- Tequila recipes

Tequila—at least on the U.S. side of the border—has long been shrouded in disreputable myth. The truly callow still regard it as a hallucinogen—rendered particularly vile by the inclusion of a worm in the bottle—but, even among more sophisticated drinkers, tequila often has a reputation as a crude, harsh beverage redolent of raw yeast and industrial solvent.

The mistaken idea that tequila is a hallucinogen comes from confusing it with another spirit, *mescal*, which, like tequila, is made from the *agave* plant (a spineless cactus), albeit a different species. But all mescal shares with *mescaline*—which is a true hallucinogen—is the first two syllables. The origin of mescal is agave, whereas mescaline comes from *peyote*.

As for that worm, you may find it in mescal, but, by Mexican law, never in tequila.

The Tequila Pedigree

Far from being a crude or crudely made drink, the manufacture of tequila is meticulously regulated by Mexican law. True tequila is distilled exclusively from mash derived from the blue agave, a plant that grows slowly and that is cultivated only in a strictly defined region surrounding the town of Tequila in the Mexican state of Jalisco. Agave hearts are harvested, roasted, shredded, and then fermented and double distilled. From here, it may be bottled or aged.

Like rum, tequila takes on its character from the plant in which it originates and from the way it is processed. Therefore, many variations in taste are possible. Sample the various tequila brands imported into this country and choose your favorite. Whatever the brand, however, there are two basic varieties: white and gold. White tequila is unaged and bottled immediately after distillation. The gold, which sometimes shades into the brown range, called *tequila añejo*, is aged in oak casks. It acquires its color just as whiskey does, from the chemical interaction with the oak.

The difference between white tequila and tequila añejo is immediately apparent to the drinker. The aged product is much smoother and mellower, and the longer it has aged, the smoother and mellower it will be. It also costs more. White tequila is not a sipping drink. Either mix it or take it as a shooter, with salt and a lime wedge. Tequila añejo, however, may be mixed or savored slowly all by itself, like whiskey or cognac.

Buzzed Words

Tequila añejo is tequila that has been aged in oak casks, acquiring a gold coloring. Unaged tequila is clear and called white tequila.

Tequila Estilo Pancho Villa, Por Favor!

Walk into any *cantina*, belly up to the bar, and demand *Tequila estilo Pancho Villa, por favor!* What you'll get is a traditional tequila shooter—the way the legendary revolutionary bandit liked it. Which goes like this:

1. Pour a shot—a jigger—of white tequila into a shot glass.

2. Take a lime wedge between the thumb and forefinger of your left hand. (Unless you're left-handed. You're doing the shot with your good hand.)

3. Put a liberal pinch of coarse kitchen salt (not fine table salt) directly behind the held wedge, in the little hollow on the back of your hand between the base of your thumb and the base of your forefinger. (It helps to lick your hand first, so the salt stays put.)

4. Pick up the shot of tequila in your right hand.

5. Lick the salt, immediately down the tequila in a gulp, and then suck the lime.

Some people call this shot a Snakebite. Whatever you call it, feel free, at this point, to bang the bar several times as you struggle to resume respiration.

Con Sangrita

Pancho Villa was used to being chased. Chase the tequila shooter with *sangrita*, a traditional Mexican concoction without alcohol. It is available premixed in stores that specialize in Mexican foods, or you can mix your own.

Sangrita

Yields 3¹/₂ cups.

2 cups tomato juice

1 cup orange juice

2 oz. lime juice

2 tsp. Tabasco sauce (or to taste)

2 tsp. very finely minced onion

2 tsp. Worcestershire sauce (or to taste)

3 pinches white pepper

Pinch celery salt (to taste)

Combine all ingredients in a blender. Blend thoroughly, and then strain into a container for chilling in the refrigerator.

The Margarita: Everybody's Favorite Tequila Cocktail

No need to cook a Mexican meal to find an excuse for a Margarita, although it is the perfect complement to one. Whatever you do, remember: the colder, the better.

Margarita

Serve in a chilled cocktail glass, optionally rimmed with coarse salt.

1½ oz. tequila (white or gold)

½ oz. triple sec

Juice of ½ large lime (or whole small lime)

Coarse salt

Lime slice

Combine all ingredients except lime slice in a shaker with ice. Shake vigorously, and then strain into the serving glass. Garnish with lime slice.

Bar Tips

Traditionally, bartenders rim margarita glasses with coarse salt. (See Chapter 2 for information on how to rim a glass.) Many drinkers find a 50/50 mixture of salt and sugar more palatable. Try it.

Frozen Margarita

Serve in a large, chilled cocktail glass or large chilled wine goblet rimmed with salt.

1 1/2 oz. white tequila   Coarse salt

1/2 oz. triple sec   Lime slice

1 oz. lemon or
lime juice

Put approximately 2 cups of cracked ice in a blender. Add all ingredients except salt and lime slice. Blend until slushy. The mixture should be firm rather than watery. Pour into the serving glass. Garnish with lime slice.

Frozen Fruit Margarita

Serve in a large, chilled cocktail glass or wine goblet rimmed with salt.

1 1/2 oz. white tequila   Dash Rose's lime juice

1/2 oz. triple sec   Coarse salt

1/2 oz. sour mix   Lime slice

Fresh fruit to taste

1 oz. fruit liqueur to harmonize with fresh fruit chosen

Put approximately 2 cups of cracked ice in a blender. Add all ingredients except salt and lime slice. Blend until slushy. The mixture should be firm rather than watery. Pour into the serving glass. Garnish with lime slice.

Blue Margarita

Serve in a large, chilled cocktail glass or wine goblet rimmed with salt.

2 oz. white tequila

³/₄ oz. blue curaçao

2 oz. sour mix

¹/₂ oz. lime juice

Coarse salt

Lime slice

Combine all ingredients except salt and lime slice in a shaker with ice. Shake vigorously, and then strain into the serving glass. Garnish with lime slice.

Strawberry Margarita

Serve in a wine goblet.

1¹/₂ oz. tequila

¹/₂ oz. triple sec

¹/₂ oz. strawberry schnapps (may substitute a strawberry liqueur)

1 oz. lime juice

6 strawberries (if desired)

In a shaker or blender with cracked ice combine all ingredients except strawberries. Shake or blend, and then pour into serving glass. Garnish with strawberries.

Top-Shelf Margarita

Serve in a chilled cocktail glass rimmed with salt.

1½ oz. gold tequila	1 oz. lime juice
½ oz. Grand Marnier	Coarse salt
1 oz. sour mix	Lime slice

Combine all ingredients except salt and lime slice in a shaker with ice. Shake vigorously, and then strain into the serving glass. Garnish with lime slice.

More Classics

Why stop with Margaritas? Here are three popular classics.

Sneaky Pete

Serve in a chilled cocktail glass.

2 oz. white tequila

½ oz. white crème de menthe

½ oz. pineapple juice

½ oz. lime or lemon juice

Lime slice

Combine all ingredients except lime slice in a shaker with cracked ice. Shake vigorously, and then pour into the serving glass. Garnish with lime slice.

Tequila Sunrise

Serve in a chilled Collins glass.

1½ oz. white or gold tequila

Juice of ½ lime

3 oz. orange juice

¾ oz. grenadine

Lime slice

Combine all ingredients except grenadine and lime slice in a shaker with cracked ice. Shake vigorously, and then pour into the serving glass. *Carefully* add the grenadine. *Do not stir!* Garnish with lime slice.

Tequila Sunset

Serve in a chilled Collins glass.

1½ oz. white tequila   Orange juice to fill

3 dashes lime juice   ½ oz. blackberry brandy

Combine tequila and lime juice in the serving glass filled with ice. Add orange juice to fill. Stir. *Carefully* pour blackberry brandy into the drink down a twisted-handle bar spoon (see Chapter 2). Allow brandy to rise from the bottom. *Do not stir!*

Citrus Mixers

Like that other tropical staple, rum, tequila marries blissfully with citrus and other fruit juices.

Matador

Serve in a chilled cocktail glass.

$1^1/_2$ oz. white or gold tequila

1 oz. lime juice

3 oz. pineapple juice

$^1/_2$ tsp. sugar syrup

Combine all ingredients in a shaker with ice. Shake vigorously, and then strain into the serving glass.

Royal Matador

Serve in pineapple shell.

1 whole pineapple

3 oz. Gold tequila

$1^1/_2$ oz. framboise

Juice of 1 lime

1 tsp. amaretto

Remove the top from pineapple and set top, with leaves, aside. Scoop out pineapple, taking care to avoid puncturing shell. Put pineapple chunks into a blender and extract the juice. Strain juice, and then pour back into blender. Add other ingredients with cracked ice. Blend thoroughly, and then serve in pineapple shell. Add additional ice to taste. Replace the top of pineapple shell and serve with long straws. This recipe makes two drinks.

Changuirongo

Serve on the rocks in a Collins glass.

1^1/$_2$ oz. white or gold tequila

Citrus-flavored soda

Lime or lemon wedge

Combine tequila and soda over ice in the serving glass. Garnish with fruit wedge.

Tequila, Liqueur, and Dash of Oblivion

Get brave by adding Kahlua or try anisette with your tequila.

Brave Bull

Serve in a chilled old-fashioned glass.

1^1/$_2$ oz. white tequila

^{3}/$_4$ oz. Kahlua

Lemon twist

Combine all ingredients except twist in a shaker with cracked ice. Shake vigorously, and then pour into the glass. Garnish with twist.

Crazy Nun

*Serve in an old-fashioned glass filled
with finely crushed ice.*

1¹/₂ oz. white or gold tequila

1¹/₂ oz. anisette

Combine all ingredients in the serving glass
filled with finely crushed ice. Stir well.

Tequila with Rum—*Yes*, Rum

Like your tequila and your rum? Have them both.
Or, just get generous with the bitters.

Berta's Special

Serve in a chilled tall Collins glass.

2 oz. tequila

Juice of 1 lime

1 tsp. sugar syrup (may substitute honey)

Liberal dashes orange bitters

1 egg white*

Lime juice

Club soda to fill

Combine all ingredients except club soda in a
shaker with cracked ice. Shake vigorously, and
then pour into the serving glass. Add club soda
to fill. Garnish with lime slice.

---

* *Raw egg may be a source of salmonella bacteria. You may wish
to avoid drinks calling for raw egg yolk or egg white.*

Quick One

Man at the bar is coughing and sneezing over his tequila and orange juice.

"Sick?" asks the fellow on the next stool.

"Doc told me that the only way to kill these kinds of germs is plenty of orange juice."

"Oh, I see."

"Trouble is: How do I get *them* to drink it?"

Coco Loco

Serve in a coconut.

1 coconut	1 oz. pineapple juice
1 oz. white tequila	Sugar syrup to taste
1 oz. gin	¹/₂ fresh lime
1 oz. light rum	

Prepare coconut by carefully sawing off the top. Do not spill out coconut milk. Add cracked ice to the coconut, and then pour in liquid ingredients. Squeeze in lime juice, and then drop in the lime shell. Stir. Sip through straws.

Bar Tips

You'll find a recipe for a tequila martini—the Tequini—in Chapter 5.

As popular as it has become in the United States, tequila is still *relatively* new to American drinkers, and there is a great deal of room for new tequila inventions. In the meantime, bold bartenders and drinkers have found places for tequila in a host of trusted standbys. For example, the sour turns out to be a natural with tequila. Don't use sour mix, but lime or lemon juice instead. The Tequila Manhattan requires a premium-label tequila añejo. Go easy on the sweet vermouth. See Appendix B for a full list of classic tequila variations.

Liquid Luxuries: Brandies and Liqueurs

In This Chapter

- V.S.O.P. and other coded messages
- How brandy and liqueurs are made
- Brandy vs. cognac
- "Flavored" or "fruit" brandies and cognac recipes
- Liqueur recipes

Today, brandy—and especially its regal incarnation as cognac—is regarded with feelings ranging from respect to awe, and, like fine champagne, it has earned a place of honor as a ceremonial libation, typically reserved for special occasions. That's fine, but brandy also makes a delicious and very useful mixer in a host of drinks that you can enjoy any time.

That's VSOP, Not RSVP

Part of the brandy/cognac mystique is locked within the letters *V.O.* or *V.S.O.P.* printed on the label. You need be puzzled no longer. V.O. just stands for *very old*, but is, in fact, applied to brandies of a rather young age (as brandies go), at least four and a half years. V.S.O.P. stands for *very superior old pale* and indicates a truly old brandy, usually 10 years old or more.

Bar Tips

Unlike wine, brandy stops aging once it is removed from the wooden cask and bottled, so the bottling date is of no significance. There is also a practical limit to how long brandy may age. After about 60 years, aging becomes deterioration.

What does aging do to brandy? The effect is twofold. To begin with, there is simply something magical about consuming a drink that was prepared years ago. You're dipping, quite literally, into history. More directly, however, aging renders the flavor of brandy or cognac more complex, more subtle, more interesting, and makes the drink smoother and mellower.

Cognac—The Regal

Everything about cognac takes more time and care than the preparation of brandy. Not only are the grapes carefully cultivated and selected, but distillation is carried out in *alembics*, which are ancient devices that turn out distillate one batch at a time (in contrast to modern continuous stills, which are suited to mass production). Less expensive brandies are distilled in continuous stills rather than in the much-more-demanding alembics.

Buzzed Words

Champagne, as applied to cognac, has nothing to do with the sparkling wine. The word is French for flat, open country, and its English equivalent is *plain*.

Flavored Brandies

Calvados is an example of a *flavored brandy*—that is, a brandy based on a fruit other than the grape. The French—as well as distillers in other countries— offer a wide range of flavored or "fruit" brandies, including pear brandy (which typically comes bottled with an entire Bartlett pear inside), raspberry brandy (known as *framboise*), strawberry brandy (*fraise*), plum brandy (*mirabelle*), and cherry brandy (*kirsch*). Burgundy's *marc* is made from the *pomace* (skin and pulp) of grapes, rather than the grape juice. The result is a most aggressive and flavorful brandy.

Flavored brandies may be sipped straight or mixed to make some very tasty drinks.

Alexanders Are Great

This is the classic dessert drink. It is rich without being too sweet and makes the perfect nightcap.

Brandy Alexander

Serve in a chilled cocktail glass.

1$^1/_2$ oz. brandy

1 oz. crème de cacao

1 oz. heavy cream

Combine all ingredients in a shaker with ice. Shake vigorously, and then strain into the serving glass.

Alexander's Sister de Menthe

Serve in a chilled cocktail glass.

1$^1/_2$ oz. brandy

1 oz. white crème de menthe

1 oz. heavy cream

Combine all ingredients in a shaker with ice. Shake vigorously, and then strain into the serving glass.

Alexander's Sister Kahlua

Serve in a chilled cocktail glass.

1$^1/_2$ oz. brandy

1 oz. Kahlua

1 oz. heavy cream

Combine all ingredients in a shaker with ice. Shake vigorously, and then strain into the serving glass.

Other Brandy Delectations

The first two drinks recall an earlier age, when brandy was considered a bracing "tonic for the blood." The other drinks in this section will simply get your blood boiling.

Brandy and Soda

Serve on the rocks in a lowball glass.

1 1/2 oz. brandy

4 or 5 oz. club soda

Combine the ingredients over ice in the serving glass.

Brandy Flip

Serve in a chilled wine glass.

2 oz. brandy

1 egg*

1 tsp. sugar syrup

1/2 oz. cream (optional)

Ground nutmeg

Combine all ingredients except nutmeg in a blender with cracked ice. Blend until smooth, and then pour into the serving glass. Sprinkle with nutmeg.

* Raw egg may be a source of salmonella bacteria. You may wish to avoid drinks calling for raw egg yolk or egg white.

Sidecar

Serve in a chilled cocktail glass.

1½ oz. brandy   ½ oz. lemon juice

¾ oz. curaçao

Combine all ingredients in a shaker with ice. Shake vigorously, and then strain into the serving glass.

Stinger

Serve in a chilled cocktail glass.

1½ oz. brandy

1½ oz. white crème de menthe

Combine all ingredients in a shaker with ice. Shake vigorously, and then strain into the serving glass.

Ambulance Chaser

Serve in a chilled cocktail glass.

2 oz. cognac

¼ oz. port

1 egg yolk*

Few dashes Worcestershire sauce

Several pinches white pepper

Blend all ingredients with cracked ice and pour into serving glass.

---

* *Raw eggs may be a source of salmonella bacteria. You may wish to avoid drinks calling for raw egg yolk or egg white.*

Apricot Offerings

If apricot brandy sounds like something your maiden aunt sips when no one's looking—well, do her a favor and mix her one of the following.

Bronx Cheer

Serve in a chilled Collins glass.

2 oz. apricot brandy

6 oz. raspberry soda

Orange peel

In a chilled Collins glass combine brandy, soda, and a few ice cubes. Stir gently. Twist orange peel over the drink and drop it into the glass.

Toast

May you never lie, cheat, or drink—but if you must lie, lie in one another's arms, and if you must cheat, cheat death, and if you must drink, drink with all of us.

California Dreaming

Best served in a parfait glass.

2 oz. apricot brandy

4 oz. orange soda

1 scoop orange sherbet

Blend ingredients with cracked ice until smooth. Pour into serving glass.

Cherry Ripe

Fruit-flavored brandies make appealing ingredients in mixed drinks. Treat them like a dessert—best in generous moderation.

Cherry Blossom

Serve in a chilled cocktail glass.

1¹/₂ oz. brandy

³/₄ oz. cherry brandy (may substitute cherry liqueur)

¹/₂ oz. curaçao

¹/₂ oz. lemon juice

¹/₄ oz. grenadine

1 tsp. sugar syrup

Combine all ingredients in a shaker with cracked ice. Shake vigorously, and then strain into the serving glass. If you wish, rim the glass with brandy and powdered sugar.

Cherry Hill

Serve in a chilled cocktail glass.

1 oz. brandy

1 oz. cherry brandy (may substitute cherry liqueur)

¹/₂ oz. dry vermouth

Orange twist

Combine all ingredients except orange twist in a shaker with cracked ice. Shake vigorously, and then pour into the serving glass. Garnish with orange twist.

Peachy Potables

Something goes deliciously crazy when a peach gets into brandy.

Peach Fizz

Serve in a chilled Collins glass.

1½ oz. brandy	1 tsp. sugar syrup
1½ oz. peach brandy	Club soda to fill
½ oz. lemon juice	Fresh or brandied
1 tsp. crème de banana	peach slice

Combine all ingredients except soda and peach slice in a shaker with cracked ice. Shake vigorously, and then pour into the serving glass. Add club soda to fill, and garnish with peach slice.

Peachtree Sling

Serve in a chilled Collins glass.

1½ oz. brandy	Club soda to fill
1½ oz. peach brandy	Brandied or fresh
½ oz. lemon juice	peach slice
½ oz. sugar syrup	1 tsp. peach liqueur

Combine all ingredients except soda, peach slice, and peach liqueur in a shaker with cracked ice. Shake vigorously, and then pour into the serving glass. Add club soda to fill, and then garnish with peach slice. Spoon on peach liqueur as a float. Do not stir.

B&B for Thee

B&B is a classic combination of Benedictine and brandy—preferably premium-label cognac. It is a delicious after-dinner drink.

Another B&B favorite is the B&B Collins. Brandy works well here, but, for a special treat, use cognac.

B&B

Serve in a snifter.

1 oz. cognac (or brandy)

1 oz. Benedictine

Combine all ingredients in snifter and swirl.

B&B Collins

Serve in a chilled Collins glass.

2 oz. cognac (or brandy)

1–2 oz. lemon juice

1 tsp. sugar syrup

Club soda to fill

$^1/_2$ oz. Benedictine

Lemon slice

Combine all ingredients except soda, Benedictine, and lemon slice in a shaker with cracked ice. Shake vigorously, and then pour into the serving glass. Add club soda to fill. Carefully pour on Benedictine as a float. Do not stir. Garnish with lemon slice.

Brandy and Champagne

Gilding the lily? Perhaps. But brandy and champagne make a sophisticated and satisfying combination.

Champagne Cooler

Serve in a chilled wine goblet.

1 oz. brandy

1 oz. Cointreau

Champagne to fill

Mint sprig

Combine brandy and Cointreau in the serving glass. Add champagne to fill and stir very gently. Garnish with mint sprig.

Chicago

Serve in a chilled wine goblet rimmed with sugar.

Lemon wedge	Dash curaçao
Superfine sugar	Dash Angostura bitters
1¹/₂ oz. brandy	Champagne to fill

Run lemon wedge around the serving glass rim to moisten. Roll the moistened rim in sugar to coat. Combine brandy, curaçao, and bitters in a mixing glass with ice. Stir well, and then strain into the serving glass. Add champagne to fill.

King's Peg

Serve in a chilled wine goblet.

3 oz. cognac

Brut champagne to fill

Pour cognac into the serving glass, and then add champagne to fill.

The Delectable Alchemy of Liqueur

Liqueurs—also called cordials—occupy a realm between the manufacture of spirits and the esoteric lore of alchemy. Ounce for ounce, you won't find stronger, more compelling, or more varied flavors than those distilled into liqueur. No distilled spirit has a more varied, more venerable, or more interesting past than the liqueurs, which partake both of ancient tradition and modern top-secret technology. At least as early as the Middle Ages, cordials were concocted as tonics and sovereign cures for whatever ailed you. Over the centuries, the formulas evolved and have been passed down as jealously guarded secrets not even the CIA knows.

Bar Tips

If you or a guest spill a sticky, colored liqueur on a fancy suit or dress, immediately soak the stain with club soda. Follow with plain water, and rub a bit of Ivory bar soap directly on the stain. Rinse with cold water, and then blot dry.

Liqueur + Liquor

Combinations of liqueur with hard liquor are deceptively potent. The liqueur makes the liquor go down easy and, before you know it, you're buzzed. Enjoy—but pace yourself by drinking responsibly.

Barracuda

Serve in a carved-out pineapple shell.

¹/₂ oz. Galliano	Pineapple shell
1 oz. gold rum	Champagne to fill
1 oz. pineapple juice	Lime slice
¹/₄ oz. lime juice	Maraschino cherry
¹/₄ oz. sugar syrup	

Combine all ingredients except champagne, lime slice, and cherry in a shaker with cracked ice. Shake vigorously, and then pour into the pineapple shell. Add champagne to fill. Garnish with lime slice and cherry.

Café Kahlua

Serve in a chilled old-fashioned glass.

3 oz. Kahlua	1¹/₂ oz. gold Jamaica rum
2 oz. cream	Cinnamon stick

Combine all ingredients except cinnamon stick in a shaker with cracked ice. Shake vigorously, and then pour into the serving glass. Garnish with cinnamon stick.

Bar Tips

Serve drinks containing dairy products fresh, just as you would serve milk alone.

Grand Hotel

Serve in a chilled cocktail glass.

1½ oz. Grand Marnier

1½ oz. gin

½ oz. dry vermouth

Dash lemon juice

Lemon twist

Combine all ingredients except twist in a shaker with cracked ice. Shake vigorously, and then pour into the serving glass. Garnish with twist.

Mazatlán

Serve in a chilled cocktail glass.

1 oz. white crème de cacao

1 oz. light rum

1 oz. cream

½ oz. coconut cream

Combine all ingredients in a shaker with ice. Shake vigorously, and then strain into the serving glass.

Melon Ball

Serve on the rocks in a highball glass.

1 oz. vodka

$^1/_2$ oz. Midori melon liqueur

5 oz. orange juice

Combine vodka and Midori in serving glass filled with ice. Add orange juice and stir well.

Arctic Joy

Serve in a chilled cocktail glass.

1 oz. peppermint schnapps

1 oz. white crème de cacao

1 oz. light cream

In a shaker or blender combine all ingredients. Shake or blend, and then strain into serving glass.

Cordial Hit Parade

Here they are, the most-often requested cordials. Every bartender should be familiar with them.

Alabama Slammer Shooter

Serve in shot glasses.

1$^1/_2$ oz. sloe gin   1$^1/_2$ oz. Southern Comfort

1$^1/_2$ oz. amaretto   1$^1/_2$ oz. orange juice

Combine all ingredients in a shaker with ice. Shake vigorously, and then strain into shot glasses. Yields four shots.

Alabama Slammer Highball

Serve in a highball glass.

$^1/_2$ oz. sloe gin

$^1/_2$ oz. Southern Comfort

$^1/_2$ oz. triple sec

$^1/_2$ oz. Galliano

3 oz. orange juice

Maraschino cherry

Orange slice

Combine all ingredients except fruit in a shaker filled with ice. Shake vigorously, and then strain into the serving glass. Add more ice, if you wish. Garnish with cherry and orange slice.

Sloe Gin Fizz

Serve in a chilled Collins glass.

1 oz. sloe gin

2 oz. sour mix

Club soda to fill

Maraschino cherry

Combine sloe gin and sour mix in a shaker filled with ice. Shake vigorously, and then strain into the serving glass. Add club soda to fill, and then garnish with cherry.

Grasshopper

Serve in a chilled cocktail glass.

1 oz. green crème de menthe

1 oz. white crème de cacao

1 oz. light cream

Combine all ingredients in a blender with ice. Shake vigorously, and then strain into the serving glass.

Pink Squirrel

Serve in chilled cocktail glass.

1 oz. crème de noyaux

1 oz. white crème de cacao

1 oz. cream

Combine all ingredients in a shaker with ice. Shake vigorously, and then strain into the serving glass.

Ballylickey Dickie

Serve in chilled wine goblet.

1½ oz. amaretto

1 oz. Irish cream

1 scoop vanilla ice cream

1 oz. slivered almonds

Pinch ground nutmeg

Pinch powdered cinnamon

Maraschino cherry

Blend all ingredients except for nutmeg, cinnamon, and cherry with cracked ice until very smooth. Pour into serving glass, sprinkle with spices, and garnish with cherry.

Brandy supercharges whatever other spirit you mix it with. This makes for a drink that tends to sneak up on you. Enjoy—but know when you've had just enough.

Fires of Passion:
Hot and Flaming Drinks

In This Chapter

- Attractions of hot drinks
- Fortified coffee drinks
- How to flame drinks dramatically and safely
- Hot drink recipes

The human body is a metabolic furnace. Heat is precious to it, and what is precious feels good. That, in essence, is the attraction of hot drinks, whether it's tea, coffee, or hot chocolate. Add alcohol to a hot drink, and that thermal glow spreads, mellows, and is sustained. In the days before central heating, no self-respecting inn would fail, in wintertime, to offer toddies or mulled drinks. The flip, an American colonial favorite consisting of spirits, ale, eggs, sugar, cream, and assorted spices, was heated on demand with a "flip iron"—a poker kept hot on the fireplace grate for the purpose of heating and frothing drinks.

Here's a chapter on some hot stuff.

A Fortified Coffee Summit

The most obvious hot drink mixer is America's favorite hot beverage: coffee. The most popular fortified coffees have international themes, derived from the kind of spirit used to fuel them.

Amaretto Café (Italian Coffee)

Serve in a coffee mug.

1¹/₂ oz. amaretto

Hot coffee to fill

Whipped cream

Pour amaretto into the mug and add hot coffee to fill. Top with whipped cream.

Bar Tips

When mixing spirits with coffee, pour the spirit in first. Then add the coffee.

Roman Coffee

Serve in a coffee mug.

1¹/₂ oz. Galliano

Coffee to fill

Whipped cream

Pour Galliano into the mug. Add coffee to fill, and top with whipped cream.

Vesuvio

Serve in a coffee cup.

1 cup hot black coffee, strong

1 oz. sambuca

1 cube sugar

Fill a cup with coffee, and then float half of sambuca on top of the coffee. Do not stir! Put sugar cube in a spoon and pour the rest of sambuca into the spoon. Ignite. Carefully dip the flaming spoon into the cup, so that the sambuca float ignites. After the drink flames for a few seconds, stir to extinguish. Serve.

Café Mexicano

Serve in a coffee mug.

1 oz. Kahlua

$1/2$ oz. white or gold tequila

Hot coffee

Whipped cream (optional)

Pour Kahlua and tequila in the mug. Add coffee. Top with whipped cream, if you wish.

Café Bonaparte

Serve in a coffee mug or hot drink glass.

$1^1/2$ oz. brandy

Cappuccino to fill

Pour brandy into the serving glass, and then fill with cappuccino.

Café Marnier

Serve in a coffee mug.

1½ oz. Grand Marnier

Espresso to fill

Whipped cream (optional)

Pour Grand Marnier into the mug. Add espresso to three-fourths full. Stir and add whipped cream, if you wish.

Irish Coffee

Serve in a coffee mug.

1½ oz. Irish whiskey

1 tsp. sugar

Coffee

Whipped cream

Pour whiskey into the mug. Add sugar. Add coffee to fill and top with whipped cream.

Creamy Irish Coffee

Serve in a coffee mug.

1½ oz. Bailey's Irish Cream

Coffee to fill

Whipped cream

Pour the liqueur into the mug. Add coffee to fill and top with whipped cream.

Jamaican Coffee

Serve in a coffee mug.

1 oz. Tia Maria

$^3/_4$ oz. rum (white, gold, or dark)

Coffee to fill

Whipped cream

Grated nutmeg

Pour Tia Maria and rum into the mug. Add coffee to fill, top with whipped cream, and sprinkle with nutmeg.

Café Zurich

Serve in a coffee mug.

1$^1/_2$ oz. anisette

1$^1/_2$ oz. cognac

$^1/_2$ oz. amaretto

Coffee

1 tsp. honey

Whipped cream

Pour the spirits into the coffee mug. Add hot coffee to three-fourths full. Float a teaspoon of honey on top of the drink, and then top honey with whipped cream.

And from the American Southland, a velvety mocha.

Comfort Mocha

Serve in a mug.

1½ oz. Southern Comfort

1 tsp. instant cocoa

1 tsp. instant coffee

Boiling water to fill

Whipped cream

Combine all ingredients except whipped cream in a mug with boiling water. Top with whipped cream.

Hot Rum Drinks

Hot rum drinks have been warming hearts and gullets for centuries. Here are two favorites.

Hot Grog

Serve in a mug.

1 tsp. sugar

Juice of ¼ lemon

1½ oz. rum

Boiling water to ¾ full

Place sugar in the mug, and then add rum and lemon juice. Finally, add boiling water to three-fourths full. Stir.

Hot Buttered Rum

Serve in a mug.

1 tsp. sugar

2 oz. white, gold, or dark rum

1 tsp. butter

Boiling water to ¾ full

Put sugar and butter in the mug, and then add rum. Pour in boiling water to three-fourths full. Stir.

Buzzed Words

A **hot toddy** is any alcohol-based sweetened hot drink. It may be shortened simply to **toddy**. There is no such thing as a cold toddy.

Toddy Collection

Your Basic Hot Toddy

Serve in a mug.

1 tsp. sugar

2 oz. blended whiskey

Boiling water to ¾ full

Put sugar in the mug, and then add whiskey. Add boiling water to three-fourths full. Stir.

Hot Toddy with Bourbon

Serve in a mug.

1 tsp. sugar

3 whole cloves

Cinnamon stick

Lemon slice

4 oz. boiling water

1 oz. bourbon

Grated nutmeg

Put sugar, cloves, cinnamon stick, and lemon slice into the mug. Add 1 ounce of boiling water and stir. After letting the mixture steep for five minutes, pour in the bourbon and rest of the boiling water. Stir. Dust with nutmeg.

You may vary either of these toddies by using brandy, rum, gin, or vodka instead of blended whiskey or bourbon.

Cozy Comforters

Just about any hot drink you can make is soothing, but the following recipes will summon up visions of true nirvana.

Bar Tips

Wine and most liqueurs cannot endure boiling. The flavor as well as much of the alcoholic content will go up in steam.

Mulled Claret

Serve in a mug.

5 oz. red Bordeaux	Pinch grated nutmeg
1 oz. port	A few whole cloves
3/4 oz. brandy	Lemon twist
Pinch ground cinnamon	

Combine all ingredients in a saucepan and heat, but do not boil. Pour into the mug.

Mulled Claret Batch

Yield: 13 drinks

2 oz. honey	1 pint ruby port
1 (750 ml.) bottle red Bordeaux	1 cup brandy
	Lemon slice

In the flaming pan of a chafing dish over direct heat, dissolve honey with 1 cup water. Add Bordeaux, port, brandy, spices, and lemon. Heat over a low flame, stirring occasionally. Do not allow to boil.

Simple Mulled Cider

Serve in mugs.

3 oz. sugar	1 cinnamon stick per mug
3 pints hard cider	
4 oz. rum	Pinch allspice per mug

Combine ingredients in a pot. Heat and stir, but do not boil. Strain into the mug. The recipe yields three large or five smaller drinks.

Buzzed Words _____

Hard cider is fermented cider and, therefore, alcoholic. **Sweet cider** is nonalcoholic
apple cider.

Arson and Pytrotechnics

Few acts of mixology are more impressive than set-
ting a drink ablaze. The effect is not only theatri-
cal; done correctly, it enhances the flavor of the
drink and, most important, results in no injury to
oneself or one's guests.

Bar Tips _____

A flaming drink is _not_ to be consumed
while it is flaming! This may sound like superfluous advice. Who'd be dumb enough to
drink fire? But in some college bars and else-
where, the idea is to down a flaming drink
at once, so that the alcohol vapor burns off
above the glass, while the liquor is safely
downed. Raising a flaming drink to your
face, and then trying to drink it, is always a
very bad idea.

Countdown

Most liquor has a relatively low concentration of
alcohol. If what you're working with is 80 proof,

the liquid is only 40-percent alcohol. This means that it probably won't burn unless it is vaporized; therefore, your first step is to heat a *small* amount of alcohol before igniting it.

This said, it must be observed that *vaporized* alcohol, even at relatively low concentrations, is *very* flammable. So, before we get into the details of how to flame drinks, let's take time for a safety check:

- Use the smallest amount of liquor possible to flame drinks. For a single drink, an ounce is sufficient.

- Do not flame drinks near draperies, curtains, paper banners, bunting, streamers, or other combustible materials.

- Never heat or flame spirits in a chafing dish at the serving table. If the hot or flaming liquid should spill, you could end up burning a number of people. Instead, heating and flaming should be done on a stable cart or serving table apart from guests.

- Do not keep uncorked spirits near an open flame.

- Never add spirits into a flaming dish! There is a good chance that the vapors will ignite and the fire will blow back on you or someone else.

- Alcohol burns with a very pale flame. If the lights in the room are bright, you and your guests may not see the flame. This is not only dangerous, but insufficiently spectacular. Dim the room lights before flaming.

- Generally, alcohol burns off quickly; however, always have a sufficiently large lid on hand to cover the chafing dish in order to put out a fire gone awry.

Bar Tips

The flaming drink is definitely not child's play. *Flaming alcohol is intensely hot and can cause serious burn injuries!* In addition to safety, it is important to flame drinks properly in order to preserve as well as enhance their flavor.

Ignition and ... Lift Off!

To flame a drink successfully and safely, begin by taking a single teaspoonful of the liquor you want to flame. Warm this over a lighted match in order to vaporize some of the alcohol. Ignite the liquor in the spoon; then carefully pour the flaming alcohol over the prepared recipe. Do *not* put your face near the drink you are flaming. Stand back.

Buzzed Words

As a verb, **flambé** means to drench with liquor and ignite. The word may also be used as a noun, synonymous with flaming drink.

Flaming Rum

Rum is well suited to the *flambé* because the flaming process creates a delicious collection of concentrated natural flavors.

Burning Blue Mountain

Serve in an eggnog–style mug.

5 oz. dark Jamaican rum　Lime rind, cut up

2 tsp. powdered sugar　Lemon twist

Orange rind, cut up

Pour rum into a chafing dish and warm. Add sugar and fruit rinds. Stir to dissolve sugar, and then ignite. Ladle the drink into the serving glass and garnish with lemon twist.

Aberdeen Angus

Serve in an eggnog–style mug.

$^1/_2$ oz. lime juice

$^1/_2$ oz. heather honey

Boiling water

2 oz. scotch

1 oz. Drambuie

Into a heat-proof mug, pour lime juice and honey. Add sufficient boiling water to dissolve honey. Into a small ladle, combine the two spirits. Ignite. Pour flaming mixture into the mug. Top off with boiling water. Stir, and serve hot.

Christmas Rum Punch

Serve in a punch bowl.

6 oranges	½ gallon sweet cider
Cloves	Powdered cinnamon
1 bottle dark rum	Grated nutmeg
Sugar to taste	

Prepare oranges by sticking them with cloves, and then baking until oranges begin to brown. Slice oranges and place in a punch bowl. Add rum. Add sugar to taste. Carefully ignite and allow to burn for a few minutes before extinguishing with cider. Garnish with cinnamon and nutmeg.

Coffee Blazer

Serve in an old-fashioned glass.

1 TB. Kahlua	Sugar
1 TB. cognac	Hot coffee to fill
Lemon slice	Whipped cream

Warm Kahlua and cognac over a match or low gas flame. Moisten the rim of the serving glass with lemon slice, and then roll the rim in sugar; drop the lemon slice in the glass. Warm the glass over a low flame to melt sugar on the rim. Pour in warmed Kahlua and cognac and ignite. Extinguish with coffee. Stir well and top with whipped cream.

Flaming Brandy

Brandy is the most frequently used fuel for flamed drinks.

Big Apple

Serve in a warmed 10-oz. mug.

3 oz. apple juice

Pinch ground ginger

3 TB. baked apple

1 oz. apple brandy

Combine apple juice and ginger in a saucepan. Heat and let simmer for a few minutes. Put baked apple in the serving mug. Pour apple brandy into a ladle. Warm the ladle over a match or a low gas flame. Ignite brandy in the ladle, and then pour over baked apple. Extinguish the fire with warm ginger-spiced apple juice. Stir. Serve warm, with a spoon for eating the apple.

Hot drinks provide cozy comfort, while flaming drinks offer high drama. Either one can enhance any social occasion.

Buzzed Word Glossary

absinthe An aromatic, bitter, very strong (containing 68-percent alcohol) liqueur flavored chiefly with wormwood (*Artemisia absinthium*) and containing other botanicals—licorice, hyssop, fennel, angelica root, aniseed, and star aniseed. Famed as the favorite drink of Henri de Toulouse-Lautrec, absinthe was outlawed in many countries early in the twentieth century because of its apparent toxicity.

aging The storage of the distilled alcohol in wooden casks, most often oak. Over months or years, the wood reacts with the alcohol, imparting to it a distinctive color, aroma, and flavor.

alcoholism The medical definition and the criteria of diagnosis of this condition vary, but, in general, this complex, chronic psychological and nutritional disorder may be defined as continued excessive or compulsive use of alcoholic drinks.

apéritif A spiritous beverage taken before a meal as an appetizer. Its origin, in French, is hardly appetizing, however, originally denoting a purgative.

aquavit Aqua vitae is not to be confused with *aquavit*, which is a very strong Scandinavian liquor distilled from potatoes and grain and flavored with caraway seeds.

arrack   A strong alcoholic beverage distilled from palm sap, rice, or molasses. It is popular in the Middle and Far East and is available in larger liquor stores.

barback   An assistant or apprentice bartender, who does the bartender's scut work, including tapping beer kegs, running ice, replacing glassware, preparing and stocking garnishes, restocking shelves, and so on.

blackout   Not a loss of consciousness, but an inability to remember, even after you are sober, what you did and said while intoxicated.

blended whiskey   A blended whiskey may be a combination of straight whiskeys and neutral, flavorless whiskeys (this is true of Canadian whisky) or it may be a combination of similar whiskey products made by different distillers at different times (as in blended scotch).

blood-alcohol concentration (BAC)   The concentration of alcohol in the blood, expressed as the weight of alcohol in a fixed volume of blood. Sometimes called *blood alcohol level*, or BAL. It is used as an objective measure of intoxication.

bottled-in-bond   Whiskey that, by federal law, must be a 100-proof, straight whiskey aged at least four years and stored in a federally bonded warehouse pending sale. Not until the whiskey is sold—withdrawn from the bonded warehouse—does the distiller have to pay the federal excise tax. Beyond these requirements, the "bottled-in-bond" designation says nothing about the quality or nature of the whiskey.

branch water   Water withdrawn from the local "branch," or stream. Sadly, in most U.S. locations, this would be a risky undertaking these days, and "branch" or "branch water" is just a romantic appellation to describe what comes out of the faucet.

champagne   As applied to cognac, champagne has nothing to do with the sparkling wine. The word is French for flat, open country, and its English-language equivalent is *plain*.

cobbler   Traditionally, an iced drink made of wine or liqueur plus sugar and fruit juice.

Coffey still   *See* continuous still.

congeners   Acids, aldehydes, esters, ketones, phenols, and tannins that are byproducts of fermentation, distillation, and aging. These "impurities" may contribute to the character and flavor of the spirit, but they cause undesirable effects in some people, notably increasing the intensity of hangover.

continuous still   Also called a Coffey still, after the inventor, Aeneas Coffey. A type of still for whiskey distillation that allows for continuous high-volume production, as opposed to the *pot still*, which must be emptied and "recharged" one batch at a time.

cordial   In modern usage, a synonym for *liqueur*; however, the word originally designated only those liqueurs thought to have tonic or medicinal efficacy.

daiquiri   A rum, lime juice, and sugar drink named after the Cuban town near the original Bacardi rum distillery.

daisy A whiskey- or gin-based drink that includes some sweet syrup and a float of—usually golden—liqueur.

distilling The process of evaporating the alcohol produced by fermentation, and then condensing the evaporated fluid to concentrate and purify it. The increase in alcohol concentration is usually great.

dry gin You will often encounter the expression *dry gin* or *London dry gin* on bottle labels. These designations originated when gin was widely available in "sweet" (called *Old Tom*) as well as "dry" forms. Today, the distinction is mainly superfluous, because almost all English and American gin is now dry. Also note that a gin does not have to be made in London or even in England to bear the "London dry gin" designation on its label. This describes a manufacturing style, not a place of origin.

dry martini A martini with relatively little vermouth versus gin. Some drinkers prefer 12 parts gin to 1 part vermouth, while others insist on a 20-to-1 ratio. Extremists do away with the vermouth altogether and have a gin and olive on the rocks.

DUI or DWI In some jurisdictions, drunk driving is called driving under the influence—*DUI*—in others, it's driving while intoxicated—*DWI*.

ethyl alcohol The potable alcohol obtained from the fermentation of sugars and starches. For producing hard liquor, the ethyl alcohol is purified and concentrated by distillation.

fermenting The chemical process whereby complex organic substances are split into relatively simple compounds. In the manufacture of alcohol, special yeasts are used to ferment—convert—the starches and sugars of grain (or some other organic substance) into alcohol.

fizz   Any drink made with soda and a sweetener.

flambé   As a verb, *flambé* means to drench with liquor and ignite. The word may also be used as a noun, synonymous with flaming drink.

flip   A drink containing liquor, sugar, spice, and egg. Often served hot. Flips were most popular in the eighteenth and nineteenth centuries.

fortified wine   A fermented wine to which a distilled spirit, usually brandy, has been added. Brandy itself is often considered a fortified wine.

freeze   A frozen drink.

garbage   A bit of fruit or vegetable added to a drink primarily for the sake of appearance. It does not significantly enhance the flavor of the drink.

garnish   A bit of fruit or vegetable added to a drink principally to enhance its flavor.

generic liqueurs   Liqueurs prepared according to standard formulas by a number of distillers.

grog   Originally, grog was nothing more than rum diluted with water and rationed to sailors of the eighteenth-century Royal Navy. Its namesake was Admiral Edward Vernon (1684–1757), who first ordered the ration. Vernon's nickname was Old Grogram, after his habit of wearing a grogram (coarse wool) cloak.

hard cider   Fermented—and therefore alcoholic—apple cider.

hard liquor   A beverage with a high alcoholic content. Gin, vodka, bourbon, sour mash whiskey, scotch, blended whiskey, rye, rum, and tequila are the most common "hard liquors."

jigger   The glass or the metal measuring cup used to measure drinks. It is also what you call the amount the jigger measures: $1^1/_2$ ounces.

light whiskey   Whiskey distilled at a high proof (in excess of 160 proof) and aged in used charred oak barrels. Light whiskey is more flavorful than neutral spirits, but not as strongly flavored as straight whiskey. It is an important component in blended whiskey.

liquor   Any alcoholic beverage made by fermentation *and* distillation rather than fermentation alone (as is the case with wine and beer).

London dry gin   *See* dry gin.

macerate   To make soft by soaking in liquid. Applied to the production of liqueurs, maceration is a process of soaking botanicals in the distilled alcohol to extract their flavor.

malt   Grain (usually barley) that has been allowed to sprout. Used as material for fermentation to produce beer or certain distilled spirits.

malting   The practice of allowing the grain (usually barley) to sprout before fermentation. In whiskey production, this produces a variety of characteristic flavors in the finished product.

mash   The fermentable starchy mixture from which an alcoholic beverage is produced.

master blender   The craftsperson in charge of selecting and proportioning the component whiskies that make up a blended whiskey.

mixed-grain whiskey   Whiskey distilled from a mash in which no single type of grain predominates. Contrast straight whiskey, which is made from mash containing at least 51 percent of a certain grain.

muddle   To mash and stir. One muddles such things as mint leaves and other solids in order to make a suspension or a paste with fluid. A special pestle-like wooden *muddler* can be used, but any spoon will do.

muddler   *See* muddle.

mull   To heat and spice a drink. Traditionally, the heating was done by inserting a hot poker into the drink; today, *mulled* drinks are usually heated on a stove.

Old Tom   A special form of gin, slightly sweetened. It is not widely enjoyed today and may be quite hard to find.

pony   Strictly speaking, a 1-ounce measure; however, pony glasses range in capacity from 1 to 2 ounces.

port (also called *porto*)   Named after the Portuguese town of Oporto, birthplace of this fortified wine and the origin of "true" port today—though other regions also produce port wines. Port is sweet, whereas sherry ranges from dry to sweet.

posset   A traditional English drink made with sweetened milk that has been curdled by the addition of wine or ale. It is usually served hot.

pot still   *See* continuous still.

pousse-café   A drink made with two or more liqueurs and, sometimes, cream. The different spirits vary in specific gravity, and therefore they float in discrete layers if carefully combined. The layered effect is novel and pretty.

proof   The alcoholic content of a spirit. It is determined by multiplying the percentage of alcoholic content by two, so that liquor that is 40-percent alcohol is 80 proof.

proprietary liqueurs   "Brand-name" products prepared according to closely guarded trade-secret formulas that are the property of specific distillers.

rickey   Any alcohol-based drink with soda water and lime—and sometimes sugar.

sangria   A cold drink made with red (sometimes white) wine mixed with brandy, sugar, fruit juice, and soda. Its blood-red color and red-blooded robustness are underscored by the meaning of the word in Spanish: the act of bleeding.

schnapps   A word used to describe any number of strong, dry liquors, but recently has been applied to a variety of flavored liqueurs. The word derives from the German original, spelled with one *p* and meaning "mouthful."

scut work   The menial chores behind the bar, such as tapping beer kegs, running ice, stocking shelves, and so on; often performed by a *barback*.

sherry   A fortified Spanish wine with a nutlike flavor. Its name is an Anglicization of Jerez, a city in southwestern Spain, where sherry was first produced and from which region the most highly respected sherry still comes.

shooter   A drink meant to be downed in a single shot, often accompanied by table banging and gasps of pleasurable pain.

sling   Any brandy, whiskey, or gin drink that is sweetened and flavored with lemon.

sloe gin   Despite the name, *sloe gin* is not a gin at all, but a sweet liqueur. Its principal flavoring is the sloe berry, the small, sour fruit of the blackthorn.

specific gravity   Applied to liquids, *specific gravity* is the ratio of the mass of the liquid to the mass of an equal volume of distilled water at 39-degrees Fahrenheit.

spirits (or *spirit*)   A generic term for an alcoholic beverage based on distilled *liquor.*

spritzer   A combination of wine—usually Rhine wine or other white wine—and club soda or seltzer. The word comes from the German for *spray.*

still   A device for distilling liquids (including alcohol) to concentrate and purify them. In its simplest form, it consists of a vessel in which the liquid is heated to vapor, a coil (or other apparatus) to cool and condense the vapor, and a vessel to collect the condensed vapor (called the distillate). Stills are made in a great many varieties, ranging from small batch stills to huge industrial continuous stills, capable of producing large volumes of distillate.

straight whiskey   The term *straight whiskey* is not to be confused with ordering "whiskey, straight" (that is, "neat," with neither ice, water, nor a mixer). The mash for straight whiskey contains at least 51 percent of a certain grain: straight malt whiskey mash contains 51-percent barley; straight rye, 51-percent rye; and straight bourbon, 51-percent corn; however, straight corn whiskey is made from mash that contains 80-percent corn.

surface tension A molecular property of liquids by which the surface of the liquid tends to contract, taking on the characteristics of a stretched elastic membrane.

sweet cider Nonalcoholic apple cider.

tequila añejo Tequila that has been aged in oak casks. It acquires a deep gold coloring and is therefore often called gold tequila; however, not all gold tequila is aged. Unaged tequila is clear and called *white* tequila.

toddy A hot drink consisting of liquor—often rum—water, sugar, and spices.

whiskey versus whisky American and Irish distillers spell the word with an *e*, while Scotch and Canadian distillers jump right from the *k* to the *y*.

wort A soluble starch in the form of an infusion of malt. It is used in the fermentation processes of making whiskey and beer.

Last Call

The recipes presented in the main body of this book are all tried and all true. For the more adventurous bartender and drinker, however, we have collected some very intriguing new or out-of-the-ordinary drinks.

This is the place to come when you're stumped behind the bar, or just looking for something unusual to knock the socks off your guests. You've become familiar with most of the recipes commonly associated with each spirit. Now explore some variations on the original recipe—or stroll down entirely new avenues with intoxicating combinations like Between the Sheets, the Accountant's Cocktail, or the impressive Loma Loma Lullaby.

Walk on the Wild Side

Some of the following are new, some not so new, but all are—shall we say—highly stimulating. They are not for the scotch-and-water or Whiskey Sour crowd.

B-52

Serve straight up in a shot glass.

$1/2$ oz. Grand Marnier

$1/2$ oz. Bailey's Irish Cream

$1/2$ oz. Kahlua

Combine ingredients in a mixing glass, stir, and then pour into the shot glass.

Bahama Mama

Serve in a chilled Collins glass.

Dash grenadine

$1^1/2$ oz. light rum

$1^1/2$ oz. gold rum

$1^1/2$ oz. dark rum

2 oz. sour mix

1 oz. pineapple juice

$2^1/2$ oz. orange juice

Maraschino cherry

Orange slice

Put a dash of grenadine in the bottom of the serving glass and set aside. Combine all other ingredients except cherry and orange slice in a shaker filled with ice. Shake vigorously, and then pour into the serving glass. Garnish with the cherry and orange slice.

Accountant's Cocktail

Serve straight up in a cocktail glass.

1 oz. sloe gin

1 oz. bourbon

1 TB. Pineapple juice

Combine ingredients in shaker with cracked ice. Shake, and then strain into serving glass.

Jell-O Shots

Serve solid and eat with a spoon, or serve semigelatinous in shot glasses.

12 oz. vodka

6 oz. Jell-O gelatin mix (choose flavor)

12 oz. water

Combine 6 ounces vodka with 6 ounces water in a saucepan. Bring to a boil and stir in Jell-O gelatin mix. Remove from stove and add remaining 6 ounces of water and 6 ounces of vodka. Let set in the refrigerator overnight.

Note: Whether in fully gelled or in semiliquid/semigelatinous form, this drink tends to retard the body's absorption of the alcohol, making it more difficult to tell when you have had "enough."

Apocalypse Cocktail

Serve straight up in a cocktail glass.

1 1/2 oz. vodka

1 oz. calvados

1/2 oz. cognac

Combine ingredients in shaker with cracked ice. Shake, and then strain into serving glass.

Long Island Iced Tea

Serve in a chilled Collins glass.

$^1/_2$ oz. gin	$^1/_2$ oz. white crème de menthe
3 oz. sour mix	
$^1/_2$ oz. vodka	Cola
$^1/_2$ oz. white tequila	Lemon wedge
$^1/_2$ oz. light rum	Mint sprigs

Combine all ingredients except cola, lemon wedge, and mint sprig with cracked ice in a blender. Blend well, and then pour into the serving glass. Add cola to fill, and garnish with lemon wedge and mint sprig.

Einstein's Brain

Serve straight up in a cocktail glass.

$1^1/_2$ oz. vodka	1 drop cherry brandy
$1^1/_2$ oz. gin	1 tsp. grenadine

Combine vodka and gin in shaker with cracked ice. Shake, and then strain into serving glass. Add brandy and grenadine.

Midori Sour

Serve in a chilled whiskey sour glass.

2 oz. Midori

1 oz. lemon juice

1 tsp. sugar syrup

Combine all ingredients in a shaker with ice. Shake vigorously, and then strain into the serving glass.

Sex on the Beach

Serve on the rocks in a highball glass.

1½ oz. vodka

1 oz. peach schnapps

Cranberry juice to three-fourths full

Orange juice to fill

Combine all ingredients in the serving glass full of ice. Stir.

Suburban

Serve on the rocks in an old-fashioned glass.

1 oz. blended whiskey

1 oz. rum

2 tsp. port wine

2 dashes Angostura bitters

2 dashes orange bitters

Combine in a shaker with cracked ice. Shake, and then strain into serving glass over a few ice cubes.

Blue Shark

Serve on the rocks in an old-fashioned glass.

1½ oz. tequila

1½ oz. vodka

½ oz. blue curaçao

Combine in a shaker with cracked ice. Shake, and then strain into serving glass over a few ice cubes.

More Joys of Gin

Dubonnet Cocktail

Serve straight up or on the rocks in a chilled old-fashioned or lowball glass.

1¹/₂ oz. gin

1¹/₂ oz. Dubonnet rouge

Lemon twist

Vigorously shake gin and Dubonnet, with ice, in a shaker; pour into the serving glass. Garnish with lemon twist.

Anita's Satisfaction

Serve in a chilled cocktail glass.

1¹/₂ oz. dry gin

Several dashes grenadine

Several dashes Angostura bitters

Several dashes orange bitters

In a shaker, mix all ingredients with cracked ice. Strain into the serving glass.

Gin Cobbler

Serve in an old-fashioned or lowball glass.

| 2 oz. gin | Club soda to fill |
| 1 tsp. orgeat syrup | Orange slice |

Stir gin and orgeat (a sweet flavoring of orange and almonds—with the accent on the almonds) in the serving glass with ice; cracked ice works best. Fill with club soda. Garnish with orange slice.

Kyoto Cocktail

Serve in a chilled cocktail glass.

1¹/₂ oz. gin   ¹/₂ oz. melon liqueur

¹/₂ oz. dry vermouth   Dash lemon juice

In a shaker or blender, mix all ingredients with cracked ice. Strain into serving glass.

The Vider Vorld of Vodka

Anna's Banana

Serve in a chilled wine glass.

1¹/₂ oz. vodka

1¹/₂ oz. lime juice

¹/₂ small ripe sliced banana

1 tsp. orgeat syrup (may substitute honey)

Lime slice

In a blender, combine all ingredients except lime slice. Blend with cracked ice until smooth. Strain into serving glass, and garnish with lime slice.

Cosmopolitan

Serve in a cocktail glass.

³/₄ oz. vodka   ¹/₂ oz. lime juice

1 oz. cranberry juice   Lemon twist

¹/₂ oz. triple sec

Shake all ingredients with ice; serve up in a cocktail glass. Garnish with a lemon twist.

Bottom Line

Serve on the rocks in a highball glass.

1¹/₂ oz. vodka   Tonic water

¹/₂ oz. Rose's lime juice   Lime slice

In a highball glass, mix vodka and lime juice with ice cubes. Fill with tonic water, and garnish with lime slice.

Cortina Cup

Serve in a chilled cocktail glass.

1 oz. vodka

¹/₂ oz. white crème de cacao

¹/₂ oz. sambuca

¹/₂ oz. heavy cream

In a blender combine all ingredients with cracked ice. Blend until smooth, and then strain into the serving glass.

Russian Wolfhound

Serve in a chilled, salt-rimmed wine goblet.

2 oz. bitter lemon soda

Salt

1¹/₂ oz. vodka

2 oz. grapefruit juice

Moisten the rim of the chilled wine goblet with bitter lemon soda, and then roll the rim in salt. Place several ice cubes in the goblet; then add vodka, grapefruit juice, and the rest of the lemon soda. Stir.

More of the Good Stuff from Kentucky and Tennessee

Bourbon Cooler

Serve in a chilled Collins glass.

3 oz. bourbon	Club soda to fill
$^1/_2$ oz. grenadine	Pineapple stick
1 tsp. sugar syrup	Orange slice
Few dashes peppermint schnapps	Maraschino cherry
Few dashes orange bitters (optional)	

Combine all ingredients except club soda and fruit in a shaker with cracked ice. Shake vigorously, and then pour into the serving glass. Fill with club soda. Garnish with fruit.

Champagne Julep

Serve in a Collins glass.

6 mint leaves

1 tsp. sugar syrup

3 oz. bourbon

Brut champagne

Mint sprig

In the bottom of the serving glass, *muddle* (stir and mash) six mint leaves in sugar syrup. Fill glass two thirds with cracked ice. Add bourbon. Stir vigorously. Add champagne to fill. Garnish with mint sprig.

Hawaiian Eye

Serve in a chilled highball glass.

$1^1/_2$ oz. bourbon

$1^1/_2$ oz. crème de banane

1 oz. Kahlua

3–4 oz. pineapple juice

1 oz. heavy cream

Dash of Pernod

1 egg white*

Pineapple slice

Cherry

Except for the fruit, combine all ingredients with cracked ice in a shaker or blender. Shake vigorously or blend at high speed for 20 seconds. Pour into serving glass, and garnish with the fruit.

* Raw egg may be a source of salmonella bacteria. You may wish to avoid drinks calling for raw egg yolk or egg white.

Whiskey Cobbler

Serve in a goblet or large snifter.

1 tsp. sugar syrup

1 tsp. orgeat syrup or amaretto liquor

2 oz. blended whiskey

Dash curaçao

Mint sprig

Fill the goblet or snifter with crushed ice. Add sugar and orgeat (or amaretto). Stir well. Add whiskey. Stir again, so that frost forms on the outside of the serving glass. Dash on curaçao and garnish with mint sprig.

Kentucky Champagne Cocktail

Serve in a chilled wine goblet with a few ice cubes.

1 oz. 100-proof bourbon

$^1/_2$ oz. peach liqueur

Few dashes bitters

Champagne

Peach slice

Combine bourbon, peach liqueur, and bitters in a chilled wine goblet with a few ice cubes. Stir, and then fill the goblet with champagne and garnish with peach slice.

'Round the Blend—Again

Frisco Sour

Serve in a sour glass.

$1^1/_2$ oz. blended whiskey

$^3/_4$ oz. Benedictine

1 tsp. lemon juice

1 tsp. lime juice

Dash grenadine

Orange slice

Combine all ingredients except orange slice in a shaker with ice. Shake vigorously, and then strain into the serving glass. Garnish with orange slice.

Horse's Neck

Serve in a Collins glass.

1 lemon

3 oz. blended whiskey

Ginger ale to fill

Peel lemon in one continuous strip and place it in the serving glass. Fill the glass one third with ice cubes. Add whiskey. Squeeze a few drops of lemon juice over whiskey, and then add ginger ale to fill.

Back to the Highlands and the Old Sod

The Minch

Serve in a chilled old-fashioned glass.

1½ oz. scotch

1 tsp. peppermint
schnapps

Club soda

Peppermint stick or candy cane
(for garnish, if desired)

Pour the scotch and schnapps into a shaker or blender with cracked ice. Shake or blend, and then pour into serving glass. Fill with club soda and add ice to taste, if desired. May garnish with a peppermint stick or candy cane.

Flying Scot

Serve in a chilled old-fashioned glass.

1¹/₂ oz. scotch

1 oz. sweet vermouth

Few dashes sugar syrup

Few dashes Angostura bitters

Combine all ingredients in a shaker with cracked ice. Pour into the serving glass.

Invercauld Castle Cooler

Serve in a chilled highball glass.

1¹/₂ oz. scotch

1 oz. Benedictine

Ginger ale

Combine scotch and Benedictine in the serving glass. Add a few ice cubes. Top off with ginger ale. Stir gently.

Royal Rob Roy

Serve in a chilled cocktail glass.

1¹/₂ oz. scotch

1¹/₂ oz. Drambuie

¹/₄ oz. dry vermouth

¹/₄ oz. sweet vermouth

Maraschino cherry

Combine all ingredients except cherry in a shaker with cracked ice. Shake vigorously, and then strain into the serving glass and garnish with cherry.

Rum Round Two

Cocoa-Colada

Serve in a chilled Collins glass.

1¹/₂ oz. Myers's rum

1 oz. Kahlua

2 oz. pineapple juice

1 oz. cream of coconut

Orange slice

Combine all ingredients except orange slice in a blender with a scoop of crushed ice. Blend until smooth, and then pour into the serving glass and garnish with orange slice.

Frozen Daiquiri

Serve in a chilled cocktail glass or in an American-style (saucer) champagne glass.

2 oz. light rum

¹/₂ oz. lime juice

1 tsp. sugar

Combine all ingredients in a blender with at least 4 ounces of crushed ice. Blend at low speed until snowy, and then pour into the serving glass.

Nutty Colada

Serve in a chilled Collins glass.

2 oz. amaretto

1 oz. gold rum

1¹/₂ oz. cream of coconut

2 oz. pineapple juice

Pineapple slice

Combine all ingredients except pineapple slice in a blender with a scoop of crushed ice. Blend until smooth, and then pour into the serving glass and garnish with pineapple slice.

Pensacola

Serve in a chilled champagne glass.

1¹/₂ oz. light
Barbados rum

1¹/₂ oz. guava nectar

1¹/₂ oz. orange juice

1¹/₂ oz. lemon juice

1 tsp. La Grande
Passion liqueur
(if desired)

Blend all ingredients in a blender until smooth. Pour into the serving glass.

Loma Loma Lullaby

Serve in a chilled Whiskey Sour glass.

1¹/₂ oz. light rum

1 oz. passion
fruit syrup

1 oz. lime juice

¹/₂ egg white

1 tsp 151-proof
Demerara rum

Combine all ingredients except Demerara rum with cracked ice in a blender. Blend until smooth, and then pour into serving glass. Float Demerara rum on top. Do not stir!

Rum Collins

Serve in a chilled Collins glass.

2 oz. light rum

1 oz. sugar syrup

$^1/_2$ lime

Club soda to fill

Combine rum and sugar syrup in the serving glass. Stir. Squeeze in lime juice, and then drop in peel as garnish. Add a few ice cubes and club soda to fill.

Rum Old-Fashioned

Serve in a chilled old-fashioned glass.

1 tsp. sugar syrup	3 oz. gold rum
Splash water	Orange twist
Liberal dashes Angostura bitters	Lime twist

Combine sugar syrup and water in the serving glass. Stir. Add bitters and rum. Stir, and then add several ice cubes. Garnish with twists.

Rampart Street Parade

Serve in a chilled cocktail glass.

1 oz. light rum

$^3/_4$ oz. crème de banane

$^1/_2$ oz. Southern Comfort

1 oz. lime juice

In a shaker or blender combine all ingredients with cracked ice. Shake or blend, and then strain into the serving glass.

Pirate's Julep

*Serve in a chilled, large old-fashioned glass
or other large glass.*

6 mint leaves

1 tsp. orgeat syrup

Few dashes Peychaud's bitters
(may substitute Pernod)

3 oz. gold Jamaica rum

1 tsp. curaçao

Mint sprig

Powdered sugar

Muddle (mash and stir) mint leaves with orgeat
in the serving glass. Dash in bitters. Fill glass
with crushed ice, and then pour in rum. Stir
vigorously until the glass frosts, adding more
crushed ice as needed. When glass is thoroughly frosted, add curaçao. Do not stir! Dust
mint sprig with powdered sugar and use the
sprig to garnish the drink.

Scorpion

Serve in a chilled wine goblet.

2 oz. light rum	1½ oz. lemon juice
1 oz. brandy	½ oz. orgeat syrup
2 oz. orange juice	Gardenia (if available)

Combine all ingredients except gardenia in a
blender with 3 oz. of shaved ice. Blend until
smooth, and then pour into the serving glass.
Garnish with gardenia.

Cantaloupe Cup

Serve in a chilled old-fashioned glass.

$1^1/_2$ oz. light Puerto Rican rum

$1/_3$ cup ripe diced cantaloupe

$1/_2$ oz. lime juice

$1/_2$ oz. orange juice

$1/_2$ tsp. sugar syrup

Cantaloupe slice

Blend all ingredients except for cantaloupe slice in a blender with cracked ice until very smooth. Pour into the serving glass, and garnish with a long, thin cantaloupe slice.

Mayaguez Watermelon Cooler

Serve in a chilled, large old-fashioned glass or other large glass.

2 oz. light Puerto Rican rum

1 oz. melon liqueur

$1/_2$ oz. lime juice

$1/_2$ oz. sugar syrup

1 cup seeded, diced watermelon

Lime slice

Combine all ingredients except lime slice in a blender. Blend at low speed for 15 seconds, and then pour into the serving glass. Garnish with lime slice.

Return to the Halls of Montezuma

Golden Margarita

Serve in a chilled lowball glass rimmed with salt.

2 oz. gold tequila	Coarse salt
1 oz. curaçao	Lime slice
$^3/_4$ oz. lime juice	

Combine all ingredients except salt and lime slice in a shaker with cracked ice. Shake vigorously, and then pour into the serving glass. Garnish with lime slice.

Tequila Collins

Serve on the rocks in a tall Collins glass.

1$^1/_2$ oz. white tequila	Club soda to fill
1 oz. lemon juice	Maraschino cherry
Sugar syrup to taste	

Pour tequila, lemon juice, and sugar syrup over ice in the serving glass. Stir, and then add club soda to fill. Garnish with cherry.

Chapultepec Castle

Serve in a chilled, large old-fashioned glass or other large glass.

1$^1/_2$ oz. tequila	4 oz. orange juice
1 oz. Grand Marnier	Orange slice

In a shaker or blender combine all ingredients, except orange slice, with cracked ice. Shake or blend, and then pour into the serving glass. Garnish with orange slice.

Grapeshot

Serve in a chilled cocktail glass.

1¹/₂ oz. tequila

³/₄ oz. coffee liqueur

³/₄ oz. cream

In a shaker or blender combine all ingredients with cracked ice. Shake or blend, and then strain into the serving glass.

Guadalajara

Serve in a chilled wine goblet.

1¹/₂ oz. tequila

2–3 oz. grapefruit juice

1 tsp. almond extract

Dash lime juice

Dash triple sec

Mint springs (if desired)

In a shaker or blender combine all ingredients, except mint sprigs, with cracked ice. Shake or blend, and then pour into the serving glass. If desired, garnish with mint.

Tequila Maria

Serve in a chilled, large (double) old-fashioned glass.

1½ oz. white or gold tequila

4 oz. tomato juice

Juice of ¼ lime

½ tsp. fresh grated horseradish

Liberal dashes Worcestershire sauce

Liberal dashes Tabasco sauce

Pinch white pepper

Pinch celery salt

Pinch oregano

Combine all ingredients in a mixing glass half filled with cracked ice. Stir, and then pour into the serving glass.

Tequila Stinger

Serve in a chilled cocktail glass.

1½ oz. gold tequila

¾ oz. white crème de menthe

Combine ingredients in a shaker with cracked ice. Shake vigorously, and then pour into the serving glass.

Just One More Snifter

Between the Sheets

Serve in a chilled cocktail glass.

1½ oz. cognac

1 oz. light rum

¾ oz. curaçao (may substitute triple sec)

½ oz. lemon juice

Combine all ingredients in a shaker with ice. Shake vigorously, and then strain into the serving glass.

BBC

Serve in a Collins glass half filled with ice cubes.

2 oz. blackberry-flavored brandy

Cola

Lemon slice

Into a Collins glass half filled with ice cubes, pour brandy, and then top off with cola. Garnish with lemon slice.

Blue Cool

*Serve in a chilled highball glass half filled
with ice cubes.*

1½ oz. peppermint schnapps

¾ oz. blue curaçao

Lemon-lime soda

Lemon sliced as wheel

In a chilled highball glass half full with ice
cubes combine schnapps and blue curaçao. Stir
well, and then fill with cold soda. Stir gently.
Slice lemon wheel halfway, so that it can be
slipped over the rim of the glass.

Brandy Julep

Serve in a chilled, large (double) old-fashioned glass.

6 mint leaves

1 tsp. honey

Splash water

Brandy to fill

Mint sprig

Powdered sugar

Combine mint leaves, honey, and a splash of
water in the serving glass. Muddle (mash and
stir) until the leaves are well bruised. Fill serving glass with shaved ice. Add brandy to fill.
Stir well so that glass frosts. Add additional
brandy and ice as necessary to fill. *Glass should
be full and thoroughly frosted.* Garnish with
sprigs, and then dust with powdered sugar.

Brandy Manhattan

Serve in a chilled cocktail glass.

2 oz. brandy

Dash Angostura bitters

$^1/_2$ oz. sweet or dry vermouth

Maraschino cherry

Combine all ingredients except cherry in a mixing glass one-third full of ice. Stir well, and then strain into the serving glass. Garnish with cherry.

Brandy Old-Fashioned

Serve in a chilled old-fashioned glass.

1 sugar cube

Liberal dashes Angostura bitters

Splash water

3 oz. brandy

Lemon twist

Put sugar cube in the serving glass, dash on bitters, and add a splash of water. Muddle (mash and stir) until sugar cube is dissolved. Half fill glass with ice cubes and add brandy. Garnish with twist.

Index

A

Aberdeen Angus, 187
absinthe, 84
accessories (bar). *See* tools
Alabama Slammer
  Highball, 171
Alabama Slammer
  Shooter, 171
alchemy, 168
alembics, 158
Alexanders, 159-160
Alternative Sex on the
  Beach, 51
Amaretto Café, 176
Ambulance Chaser, 162
American champagne
  glasses, 13
Angostura bitters, 31
apricot brandy, 163
Arctic Joy, 171
Atomic Bomb, 37

B

B&B (Brandy &
  Benedictine), 166
Bal Harbour Cocktail,
  107
Ballylickey Belt, 124
Ballylickey Dickie, 173
Banana Daiquiri, 134
bar mix. *See* sour mixes
bar spoons, 10
Barracuda, 169
bars
  stocked items, 1-9
  tools, 9-11, 23-25
Basic Hot Toddy, 181
Beefeater, 30
beer, 2
Benedictine & Brandy
  (B&B), 166
Bermuda Cocktail, 42
Berta's Special, 154
Between the Sheets, 139
Big Apple, 189
Biscayne Manhattan, 90
bitters
  absinthe, 84
  Berta's Special, 154
  rye recipes, 108
Black Russian, 52
Blackthorn, 122
Blackwatch, 119
blended scotch, 114
blending drinks, 24
Blood and Sand, 121
Bloody Blossom, 47-48
Bloody Mary, 46
Blue Hawaiian, 137
blue margaritas, 149
Blue Sky Martini, 65
Bluegrass Cocktail, 74-76
Bobby Burns, 121
Bombay, 30

Bow Street Special, 125
branch water, 70
brandy
    flavored, 159
    V.S.O.P., 157
Brandy Alexander, 160
Brandy and Soda, 161
Brandy Flip, 161
brandy snifters, 14
Brave Bull, 153
Brigadoon, 122
Bronx Cheer, 163
Bronx Cocktail, 37
Burning Blue Mountain, 187

C

Café Bonaparte, 177
Café Foster, 142
Café Kahlua, 169
Café Marnier, 178
Café Mexicano, 177
Café Zurich, 179
California Dreaming, 163
Calypso, 141
Canadian Old-Fashioned, 93
Candy Pants, 96
Cape Codder, 48
carbonated mixers, 3
Cayman Cup, 49
celery stalks, 9
champagne
    bottles, opening, 25-26
    glasses, 13
Changuirongo, 153
chasers, 146
cherries (maraschino), 8
Cherry Blossom, 164
Cherry Cola, 131

Cherry Hill, 164
Chicago, 167
chilling glasses, 27
Chocolate Martini, 66
Christmas Rum Punch, 188
cobblers, 74-75
cocktail glasses, 12
Cocktail Na Mara, 123
Cocktail of the Sea, 123
cocktail shakers, 10, 23
cocktail strainers, 10
cocktail straws, 9
cocktail swords, 9
cocktail toothpicks, 9
cocktails (stirred), 21
Coco Chanel, 42
Coco Loco, 155
coffee drinks, 141-142, 176-180
cognac, 158
Collins glasses, 11
Colloden Cheer, 119
Comfort Mocha, 180
comforting hot drinks, 182-183
coolers, 103
copita glasses, 13
cordial glasses, 13
cordials. See liqueurs
corks, popping, 25-26
corkscrews, 25
Cornell Cocktail, 41
Crazy Nun, 154
Creamy Irish Coffee, 178
Cuba Libre, 130
cutting boards, 11

D

daiquiris, 132-133
daisies, 39-40

Dark Bourbon Rose, 78
De Rigueur, 92
Devil, The, 111
Diamond Head, 44
Dog Sled, 98
dry gins, 30
Dry Mahoney, 80
Dry Manhattan, 88
dry martinis, 58-59
Dry Rye Manhattan, 110
Dutch gin, 30

E

eggnog mugs, 16
electric blenders, 11
European champagne
  glasses, 13
exotic liqueurs, 6

F

filtering vodka, 46
fizz glasses, 15
fizzes, 39
flaming drinks, 184
  drinking, 184
  lighting, 186
  safety, 185-186
flavored brandies, 159
flavored vodka, 46
flavoring glasses, 28
flips, 104
Flirtini, 65
flutes (champagne), 13
Foamy Sour Mix, 4
Fontainebleau Sidecar, 79
fortifiers, 106-107
Fraise, 159
Framboise, 159
Frisco Cocktail, 108

Frontenac Cocktail, 99
frosting glasses, 27
frozen drinks
  Fruit Margarita, 148
  Juleps, 73
  making, 24
  Margarita, 148
Frozen Julep, 73
Fruit Margarita, 148
Fuzzy Navel, 51

G

garbage, 7-9
garnishes, 7-9
Gimlets, 34
gins
  dry, 30
  premium brands, 30
Gin and Bitters, 31
Gin and Campari, 31
Gin Gibson, 63
Gin and Ginger, 32
Gin and Sin, 32
Gin and Soda, 33
Gin and Tonic, 33
glassware, 11-16
  flavoring, 28
  frosting, 27
  salting, 28
Godfather, The, 118
gold tequila, 144
Grafton Street Sour, 125
Grand Hotel, 170
Grand Marnier, 68
Grapefruit Cooler, 91
grapes, 159
Grasshopper, 172
Grog, 135

H

Harvey Wallbanger, 50
Hawaiian Martini, 66
highball glasses, 11
highballs, 18-19
Highland Fling with
  Milk, 117
Highland Fling with
  Sweet Vermouth, 117
Horse's Neck, 87
Hot Buttered Rum, 181
hot drinks
  coffee, 176-179
  comforting, 182-183
Hot Grog, 180
Hot Toddy, 181
Hot Toddy with Bourbon,
  182
Hunter's Cocktail, 106
Hurricane, 137

I

ice, 59
ice buckets, 11
Indian River Rye
  Cocktail, 111
Inverness Cocktail, 120
Irish Coffee, 178
Irish Fix, 124
Irish Mist, 124
Irish Rainbow, 123
Irish whiskey, 122-123

J

Jamaican Coffee, 141, 179
Javier Saavedra, 135
jiggers, 14, 18

juices, starter bars, 3
Jungle Jim, 55

K

Kamikaze, 52
King's Pen, 168
Kirsch, 159

L

Ladies' Cocktail, 97
Lemon Drop, 68
lemon twists, 8
light whiskies, 86
lighting flaming drinks,
  186
lime wedges, 8
liqueurs
  exotic, 6
  starter bars, 2
liquors, starter bars, 2
Little Dix Mix, 138
London dry gins, 30
Lord Baltimore's Cup,
  108
lover's sigh, 26
lowball glasses, 11
lowballs, 21

M

Madeira Cocktail, 98
Mai Tai, 138
Manhattan, 88
maraschino cherries, 8
Maraschino liqueur, 41
Margaritas, 147-150
martini glasses, 16

martinis
  dry, 58-59
  dry vermouth, 58
  ice, 59
  olives, 59
  secrets, 58-59
master blenders, 86
Matador, 152
Mazatlan, 170
measuring, 19
Melon Ball, 171
Millionaire Cocktail, 81
Mint Juleps, 71-72
Mirabelle, 159
mixed drinks, 7-9
mixed-grain whiskies, 86
mixers, starter bars, 3-7
muddle, 73
mugs, 15
Mulled Cider, 183
Mulled Claret, 183
Mulled Claret Batch, 183

N

Navy Grog, 136
Negroni, 32
New Yorker, 95
nonflavored vodka, 46

O

Old Pepper, 106
Old Tom gins, 30
old-fashioned drinks, 93
old-fashioned glasses, 12
Old-Fashioned
  Manhattan, 89
olives, 8, 59
onions, 8

Orange Blossom, 36
orange slices, 8
Orgasm Martini, 67
Original Sazerac, 84
Original Sex on the Beach,
  51
Outrigger, 139

P - Q

Paddy Cocktail, 126
Pale Bourbon Rose, 78
Pancho Villa (Tequila),
  145
parfait glasses, 15
paring knives, 11
peach brandy, 165
Peach Daiquiri, 134
Peach Fizz, 165
Peachtree Sling, 165
Peachtree Street, 96
pear brandy, 159
pearl onions, 8
Perfect Manhattan, 89
Perfect Martini, 62
Perfect Rye Manhattan,
  110
pilsners, 15
Piña Colada with Gold
  Rum, 132
Piña Colada with Light
  Rum, 131
Pink Lady, 44
Pink Squirrel, 173
Plantation Punch, 141
Planter's Punch, 140
plum brandy, 159
pomace (grapes), 159
pony glasses, 13

popping corks, 25-26
pouring drinks
    speed pourers, 10, 26
    three-count technique, 19
    two-finger measure, 19
pousse-café glasses, 15
Presbyterian, 82

R

raspberry brandy, 159
Really Dry Martini, 62

S

salting glasses, 28
Sangrita, 146
Saskatoon Stinger, 99
scotch, 114
    blended, 114
    single-malt, 114
Scotch Smash, 120
Screwdriver, 50
seals (cocktail shakers), 23
Sex on the Beach, 51
shakers (cocktail), 10, 23
shaking drinks, 20-23
sherry glasses, 13
shooters
    Alabama Slammer
        Shooter, 171
    Kamikaze, 52
    tequila, 145
shot glasses, 14
Sidecars, 162
    Bourbon Sidecar, 79
    Fontainebleau Sidecar, 79

Gin Sidecar, 41
    Sidecar, 162
Simple Mulled Cider, 183
Simple Sazerac, 83
Singapore Sling, 43
single-malt scotch, 114
Slings, 42
Slippery Knobs, 68
Sloe Gin Fizz, 172
smashes, 120
Smirnoff, 45
Sneaky Pete, 150
sour glasses, 12
sour mixes, 3
    recipes, 4
    tequila combinations, 156
speed pourers, 10, 26
spoons (bar), 10
starter bars, 1
Stinger, 162
stirring drinks, 20-21
stocking bars, 1
straight whiskey, 86
strainers (cocktail), 10
strawberry brandy, 159
Strawberry Daiquiri, 134
Strawberry Margarita, 149
straws (cocktail), 9
sugar syrup, 5
swizzle sticks, 9
swords (cocktail), 9
Sylvius, Franciscus, 30

T - U

Tanqueray, 30
Ten Ton Cocktail, 109
Tennessee whiskey, 73

tequila
  hallucinogen myth, 143
  margaritas, 147
  Pancho Villa, 145
  pedigree, 144
  shooters, 145
  sour mixes, 156
  white, 144
Tequila Pancho Villa, 145
Tequini, 68
three-count technique, 19
Tiger's Milk, 140
toddies, 104, 181-182
Tom Collins, 35
tools, 9-11, 23-25
toothpicks, 9
Top-Shelf Margarita, 150
two-finger measure, 19

V

vermouth and scotch combinations, 121-122
Vesuvio, 177
vodka
  filtering, 46
  flavored, 46
  martinis, 58
  nonflavored, 46
V.S.O.P., 157
Vodka Collins, 54
Vodka Gibson, 64
Vodka Tonic, 56

W-X-Y-Z

Ward Eight, 82
whiskies, 70-71
  blended, 85
  Canadian, 87
  Irish, 122-123
  light, 86
  mixed-grain, 86
  rye, 102
  straight, 86
  sour, 22-23, 94-95
  Tennessee, 73
Whiskey Curaçao Fizz, 91
Whiskey Rebellion of 1794, 69
white rum, 67
White Russian, 53
white tequila, 144
Wicklow Cooler, 126
wine glasses, 13
wines
  adding to starter bars, 6
  bottles, opening, 25
worms, 25

Yashmak, 107

Zombie, 136